AUTHORS TEENS LOVE

# Orson Scott Card

## Architect of Alternate Worlds

Edward Willett

**Enslow Publishers, Inc.**
40 Industrial Road
Box 398
Berkeley Heights, NJ 07922
USA
http://www.enslow.com

**Library of Congress Cataloging-in-Publication Data**

Willett, Edward, 1959-
Orson Scott Card: architect of alternate worlds / by Edward Willett.
p. cm. — (Authors teens love)
Includes bibliographical references and index.
ISBN 0-7660-2354-0
1. Card, Orson Scott—Juvenile literature. 2. Authors, English—20th century—Biography—Juvenile literature. 3. Young adult fiction—Authorship—Juvenile literature. I. Title. II. Series. 4. Science fiction—Authorship—Juvenile literature. 5. Fantasy fiction—Authorship—Juvenile literature. I. Title. II. Series
PS3553.A655Z95 2006
813'.54—dc22

2005020832

Printed in the United States of America

10 9 8 7 6 5 4 3 2 1

**To Our Readers:** We have done our best to make sure all Internet addresses in this book were active and appropriate when we went to press. However, the author and publisher have no control over and assume no liability for the material available on those Internet sites or on other Web sites they may link to. Any comments or suggestions can be sent by e-mail to comments@enslow.com or to the address on the back cover.

Every effort has been made to locate all copyright holders of material used in this book. If any errors or omissions have occurred, corrections will be made in future editions of this book.

**Illustrations Credits:** Bob Henderson, Henderson Photography, Inc., pp. 4, 46; University Laboratory High School Library, Urbana, IL, p. 89.

**Cover Illustration:** Bob Henderson, Henderson Photography, Inc., (inset); Corel Corporation (background).

# Contents

## Chapter 1

# The Beginning of *Ender*

In the late 1960s, a sixteen-year-old boy living in Orem, Utah, read Isaac Asimov's *Foundation* trilogy, a classic science fiction epic set in the far future.

There was nothing particularly unusual about that. Lots of teenagers read the *Foundation* trilogy in the 1960s. But this particular boy had a strong interest in writing. As a result, his reaction to the *Foundation* trilogy went beyond mere enjoyment.

"I found myself wanting to come up with a futuristic story myself," Orson Scott Card recalls.[1]

The idea he came up with was the seed of an award-winning short story published years later, which blossomed into an award-winning novel, which grew into a series of novels, and which may soon be a major motion picture. That story, "Ender's Game," and its spin-offs have struck a chord with both adult and young readers for more than thirty years.

Besides his popular books set in "The Enderverse," the fictional future of *Ender's Game*, Card has written dozens of novels, short stories, plays, audio scripts, musicals, and articles. His works range across many genres, including science fiction, political commentary, fantasy, history, and retellings of the great stories of the Bible and the Book of Mormon.

In *Ender's Game*, gifted children playing elaborate computerized war games are actually learning to fight a very real war between humans and insect-like aliens. The title comes from the name of the main character, Andrew "Ender" Wiggin.

The key to the *Ender's Game* story is something called the Battle Room, which Card describes as "a place contained within walls, so you don't lose soldiers off in space during training; but still in null-G [zero gravity] so they can get used to combat techniques."[2]

Orson Scott Card (Scott to his friends and family) came up with the Battle Room when he began casting around for an idea on which to base his futuristic story.

"Since I had been a Civil War buff for years, and because my brother Bill was in the army at the time (and the Vietnam War was at its peak), I speculated on how military training would be different in the future," Card recalls. He realized that in a war in outer space, there would be three dimensions to think about, and that, unlike in an airplane, there would be no "down" to orient to. Thus he envisioned the Battle Room, a means of training soldiers for space combat.[3]

He had his idea; what he did not have yet was a story to go with it. And he did not have one for years.

Soon after, Card found himself short of money. After obtaining a bachelor's degree in theater from Brigham Young University in 1975, he had tried creating his own theater company. Unfortunately, the company was a financial failure. He was in debt, and his job as assistant editor at *The Ensign*, the official magazine of the Church of Jesus Christ of Latter-day Saints, did not pay enough for him to live on, let alone pay off his debt. A second job as a copyeditor at Brigham Young University Press helped, but not enough.

Card had been writing for years, primarily plays. He decided to see if he could make some money writing something else. He chose the science fiction genre because he felt it paid well enough to make it worthwhile, but did not pay so well that he would be competing with the top writers in the field. He figured they would all be concentrating on novels.[4]

He pulled out a short story he had submitted five years earlier to the science fiction magazine *Analog*. Called "The Tinker," it told of a tinker who had the ability to heal people's diseases and to communicate with birds. When the villagers slaughter some birds that the tinker considers his friends, he withdraws from the village, and that winter an epidemic kills many of them. The villagers blame him for the deaths and murder him.

Card thought it was science fiction, since it dealt with special mental abilities, a staple in many science fiction stories. He envisioned the world on which the story was set as one in another solar system that had been colonized by people from Earth. But when he submitted the story, the new editor of *Analog*, Ben Bova, did not agree. To him, the pastoral setting suggested a medieval fantasy. *Analog*, he told Card, did not print fantasy.[5]

However, "Apparently he saw some reason to hope that I might have some talent," Card said. "His rejection letter urged me to submit a real science fiction story, because he liked the way I wrote."[6]

Card thought he already *had* submitted a "real" science fiction story, but nevertheless he set out to write something that would *feel* more like science fiction. As he put it, "I set out to write an SF story with rivets instead of trees."[7]

He needed an idea, and he had one in hand: the concept of the Battle Room he had come up with when he was sixteen. But now, years later, he realized that the story would be more powerful if the soldiers being trained in the Battle Room were all little kids. "This . . . came out of the obvious truth that most of the time our soldiers are children, or we make them into children through training—we want them utterly dependent on their commanders for their understanding of reality, the way children are utterly dependent on their parents."[8]

Card began his new story, "Ender's Game," during an afternoon outing with a friend and her children. When it was complete, he sent it to Ben Bova at *Analog*. This time, after some tightening, Ben Bova accepted it, and the story appeared in the August 1977 issue of the magazine.

That story, by a previously unknown writer, made a splash in the world of science fiction. "Ender's Game" was nominated for a Hugo Award, the genre's top award (voted on by members of the annual World Science Fiction Convention). It did not win; but in 1978, Card won the John W. Campbell Award for Best New Writer.

Card had been right. He *could* write and sell science fiction. Over the next few years he sold many more short stories and several novels. Then, in 1983, Card's agent, Barbara Bova (wife of *Analog* editor Ben Bova), wanted Card to sell something to Tom Doherty, who had just started a new publishing company called Tor Books. That something was the outline for a novel called *Speaker of Death* (later changed to *Speaker for the Dead*).

Card began working on the book, but soon realized that to make it work he needed to include an adult version of Andrew "Ender" Wiggin. And in order to make that work, he first needed to expand Ender's story. As Card remembers:

> I happened to be going to the ABA (American Booksellers Association) convention in Dallas. Tom Doherty happened to be there. I worked up my courage and found him to be absolutely approachable. . . . Our 'meeting' consisted of walking around the ABA talking. I told him that the only way to write *Speaker for the Dead* was to first write a novel version of "Ender's Game." I thought that I was going to have to start persuading or begging, that I'd have to kneel or pray. Instead, he said, "Sounds good to me."[9]

Card went home and began to write. He wrote the first few chapters of the new novel version of *Ender's Game* in one week, then went on a book-signing trip for another of his books. When he returned, he finished the novel in three weeks. The whole book was written in December and January of 1983–1984.

When it appeared in 1985, it was an even bigger hit than the original story. It won the 1986 Nebula Award (the second-most-important award in science fiction, voted on by members of the Science Fiction Writers of America) and the 1986 Hugo Award for best novel. And then, the following year, *Speaker for the Dead*, with the adult character of Ender Wiggin, duplicated the feat.

To science fiction readers, Card seemed more or less like an overnight sensation. But in fact, the roots of Card's writing and storytelling ability go deep into his childhood.

# Chapter 2

# Early Life

Orson Scott Card was born in Richland, Washington, on August 24, 1951. He was the third child of Willard Richards Card and Peggy Jane Park Card. He had a sister, Janice, six, and a brother, four-year-old Willard (Bill) Sherman.

Just a month after Scott was born, the family moved to San Mateo, California, where Willard Card started a sign-painting company.[1] Their house in San Mateo was on Fernwood Drive, two or three houses in from Alameda de Las Pulgas, on what Card remembers as a steep hill.

"I remember as a three-year-old running on the sidewalk down [that] hill and getting away from my mom and losing control, so I fell and skinned my knees. A terrible feeling, to be running and unable to stop." And, he notes wryly, he was "too dumb at age three to think of turning aside and falling on somebody's lawn."[2]

The family did not live in San Mateo very long. Willard Card had long suffered from back problems. He had managed to serve in the Navy during the Second World War, but his back was getting worse. He eventually required surgery. That meant closing the sign-painting company—and another move for the family.[3]

When Scott was three, Willard and Peggy Card took their children, who now included a new little brother, Russell Gordon, born in October 1954, to Salt Lake City. There, Willard took classes at the University of Utah, working to complete his Bachelor of Arts degree.

Across the street in front of their Salt Lake City house was a park where the Card children played Fox and Geese on paths they tramped out in the winter snow. In dry weather they could hike up the canyon to a fountain from a natural spring; "alum" (aluminum sulfates) in the water made it sour.[4]

Later the family lived in Stadium Village on the University of Utah campus: rows of prefabricated houses were located where the university's stadium is now. His dad built a plywood partition to create a third bedroom in the crowded house and Card remembers taking baths in the sink. It was a "very lively community, full of children."[5]

Salt Lake City is the headquarters of the Church of Jesus Christ of Latter-day Saints, also known as the Mormons. Another of Card's early memories is taking walks with his grandmother down to Temple Square, a ten-acre city block on which the Salt Lake Temple, Salt Lake Tabernacle, and other buildings belonging to the church are located.[6]

Scott was immersed in the Mormon faith from the very beginning. Scott's great-great-grandfather was none other than Brigham Young,[7] who led the first pioneer Latter-day Saints west from Winter Quarters, Nebraska, (near present-day Omaha) to the Salt Lake Valley in 1847. He chose the site of the settlement that became Salt Lake City, and designated the place where the Salt Lake Temple would be built.[8]

All of Card's ancestors for at least three generations (and in some cases four or five) were members of the Mormon Church. Through the Richardses, his father's mother's family, Card is descended from three of the church's apostles. "Her family was therefore of the social crème-de-la-crème of Salt Lake City society," Card notes. His father's father's family included Charles Ora Card, who founded the Mormon colony in Cardston, Alberta, Canada, and married Zina, the most prominent daughter of Brigham Young. Charles and Zina Card's daughter, also named Zina, later married Hugh B. Brown, who became an apostle and a counselor in the church's First Presidency.

In other words, Card says, "LDS [Latter-day Saints] history and family history were the same."[9]

But that family history produced some tensions

as well. His mother's side of the family, the Parks, included early pioneers, but no one famous. Certainly it was not as well-connected within the church as the Card family. As he grew older Card realized that his father's mother, Lucena ("Nana Lu" to Scott), had been horrified when two of her children married into the Park family. Her first child, Dick, after all, had married the niece of then-apostle (and later Church President) David O. McKay, and her own father and grandfather had both been in line to be president if they had lived long enough, while her brother was an apostle.

**"LDS [Latter-Day Saints] history and family history were the same."**

**—Orson Scott Card**

"Instead," Card says, "her beloved daughter Delpha married Sherman Park, who I do not think finished college, and took her up to live on a farm in Benton City, Washington, where they raised eight kids with no money; while her strange, model-building, picture-taking son Bill married the flamboyant, red-headed, opera-singing, hot-tempered Peggy Park, Sherman's younger sister, whereupon they proceeded to have six kids and no money."

Since, in his grandmother's eyes, his aunt Delpha "could do no wrong," Card says, his grandmother's scorn for the Parks was all directed at his mother. "So many times we went to Salt Lake for General Conference [a Mormon meeting] and stayed in Nana Lu's and Grandpa's house (which we loved!), only to have the visit end with my mother in tears of rage and Nana Lu cold-faced as she stalked around the kitchen making brilliant pot roasts and horrible vegetables for us to eat."[10]

But one thing Nana Lu and Peggy (and Willard) could all agree on was their desire that Scott and his siblings grow up faithful Latter-day Saints. Many churches teach that the family is the bedrock of Christian society; one of the things that makes the Church of Jesus Christ of Latter-day Saints distinct is its teaching that the family will remain intact even after death, provided members continue to faithfully observe church teachings.[11]

For that reason, Card says, religion is a part of life in a Mormon family from the very beginning. "You have always gone to church," he says. "Your parents talk about religious things right along with secular things so you really only learn the dividing line later, when you realize there's stuff they don't want you talking about at school."[12]

One way in which this focus on family manifests itself is the once-a-week family nights. "We would act out scripture stories or learn skills like table setting or do flannel-board presentations," Card recalls. "My parents always made a big production out of it—so that when I eventually read *Little Women*, I already knew all about family theatricals."

Two other activities central to Card family life

were music and reading. "We were surrounded with music—and expected to produce it ourselves," Card remembers. His grandmother used to sing to him during their walks ("church songs and songs about the flowers planted at Temple Square"); by the time he was four, he was harmonizing with her in duets.[13]

Reading—and books to be read—also surrounded Scott. His parents taught him the alphabet. His older sister Janice taught him to read: "or at least, it was sessions of reading with her that I remember best," Card says. "I remember reading aloud to her from Nancy Drew and coming across the word 'knew' which I pronounced 'canoe'—that's when I learned about silent letters."[14]

The summer before he started first grade, Scott memorized a couple of Golden Books (the short, inexpensive books designed for early readers) and called it reading—but he did not really become a fluent reader until after he was in school.

That school was not in Salt Lake City, however. In 1957, when Scott was six years old, the family moved again, to Santa Clara, California.

# Chapter 3

# School Days

The family moved to Santa Clara so Willard Card could teach and work on his master's degree at San Jose State College.[1] Once he had his degree, he took a job developing instructional materials at Lockheed, an aerospace company.[2]

Scott attended Grades 1 to 7 in Santa Clara, then a sleepy town of pear orchards and creeks. The family lived at 975 Las Palmas Drive, one of many mirror-image, three-bedroom tract houses. When the Cards first moved there, Bill, Scott, and Russell shared one bedroom, sleeping on trundle beds. "Toward the end, when Bill got a private room, I got the top bed, but most of the time I had the middle one," Card recalls.[3]

On the other side of the easy-to-climb back fence of the family yard lay San Tomas Aquinas

Creek. Today it is covered by the San Tomas Aquinas Expressway, but in the late 1950s it was still wild. "Whenever it rained the creek would fill up at flash-flood speeds—kind of dangerous," Card says. "I was always afraid that it would overflow the banks and flood us. . . . My friends and I, though, would wander the creek beds and have adventures—never as elaborate as Tom Sawyer's fantasy life, but fun all the same. . . .

"We knew our neighbors and played hide-and-seek and freeze tag and other great games in the street or in backyards, and in the summer we played until darkness or our moms' voices called us in. A Ray Bradbury childhood."[4]

But not a perfect one, of course. "I had a reasonably happy childhood, but because misery and fear expand to fit the available events, I naturally had about as much angst as I was going to have anyway, only about more trivial events," Card says.[5]

One not-so-trivial event he recalls was a run-in with a bully shortly after the family moved to Santa Clara. Scott's path to school took him through an orchard. Near the end of the path was a bridge over a creek. High fences on both sides of the path by the bridge meant a child Scott's age could not escape it, and it was there that the bully confronted him—"an over-large kindergartner, with thick glasses—but he was bigger than me, and *way* more aggressive.

"I was terrified and had no idea what to do. It didn't even occur to me to fight him. He just ordered me not to cross the bridge. But since I had to . . . anyway, the first day I got past him, but he warned me not to come tomorrow, and I believed him. So I begged my mom to drive me. She couldn't, but she told my brother to walk with me. He, however, was too afraid of being embarrassed by walking the path to the little kids' school with his kid brother, so after walking with me to the beginning of the path, he then abandoned me there, even though I told him, crying, that the bully was inside the orchard, at the bridge. I don't think I ever forgave him for that abandonment. Because the bully was there, and started shoving me around; it took a couple of older kids who didn't even know me to pull him away. (And one of them scornfully said, 'He's a kindergartner.' I didn't know enough to answer him, 'But I'm a pacifist!')"[6]

That incident may have played a role in the subject matter of the first story Scott wrote years later.

Although he was not writing stories then, Scott was definitely reading them. "Mom had favorite books that she shared with me at a very early age," Card recalls. He read *The Bobbsey Twins*, the Thornton W. Burgess animal tales, and *Nancy Drew* mysteries; *Tom Sawyer*, *Little Women*, *Little Men*, and *Jo's Boys*; and *The Prince and the Pauper*, "which fascinated me with England and English history; I read about all the kings in a little one-volume encyclopedia." Later came *Gone with the Wind* by Margaret Mitchell ("there were scenes I was *way* not ready for, but I recovered"), and the

Williamsburg novels of Elswyth Thane—especially *Dawn's Early Light* and *Yankee Stranger*, "which really set me to dreaming." He read books by Jane Austen and Charles Dickens, mysteries and historical novels—and yes, some science fiction.

"It was my older brother who encouraged me to read science fiction—*Catseye* by Andre Norton was a book he lent to me early on," Card says. In the Santa Clara Public Library when he was eight or nine, he found anthologies of science fiction stories edited by Groff Conklin. "But it was never the majority of my reading."[7]

**"Mom had favorite books she shared with me at a very early age."**

**— Orson Scott Card**

He read nonfiction as avidly as fiction. "A book about great figures in medical history so intrigued me that for years I thought I wanted to be a doctor." At about the same time his parents gave him Bruce Catton's three-volume Civil War history, *Army of the Potomac*—"definitely not a book for children!" Card says.

"This book consumed me. It gave me a clear picture of the brutality of war, the cost of stupidity, and struggles of presidents to lead nations and find worthwhile commanders to serve under them. It also gave me a sense of what history ought to be, and a keen eye for detecting historical biases or sloppiness, for Catton was rigorous, and having seen rigor, I was much better able to detect its absence."[8]

One book that met his new Catton-inspired definition of rigorousness was *The Rise and Fall of the Third Reich* by William Shirer. When he was ten years old, his sister Janice was assigned to read it in high school, and Scott read it, too. He calls the experience "devastating." The chapter on Nazi medical experiments on Jewish prisoners made a particular impact. "That was the first time I had really confronted evil. I was deeply disturbed by the notion that men could create rational motivations for doing such things."[9]

Scott also loved maps. He memorized the globe—the names of all the countries and their capitals, the shapes of the countries, what bordered on what. He insisted on navigating on family trips, calculating mileages and seeing how the markings on the maps corresponded to the real world.

Even though his parents gave him, or pointed him to, books they thought he might be interested in, they were not entirely supportive of his reading habit. "I had a way of getting so engrossed in a book that I really didn't hear anything. Not calls to dinner, nothing. They had to come up and shake me. When they bought a set of *World Book* encyclopedias, I read them from cover to cover. I was downright antisocial, and they worried, kept encouraging me to put the book down and go outside. And sometimes I did. But I usually preferred the book, and couldn't wait to get back to it. That was me—nobody else in the family was that insane about reading."[10]

There was something else very important that Scott read during these early years. When he was about seven, his parents lent him a copy of Emma Mar Petersen's *Book of Mormon Stories for Young Latter-day Saints*. They also got a four-volume set of Bible stories "with Durer engravings—lots of nudes, which made the Flood extra fascinating." Scott devoured all of the tales, and soon graduated to the Bible and the Book of Mormon proper. In fact, he says, the Book of Mormon was probably the first adult book he read all the way through.[11]

Ever since, Card says, the Book of Mormon has been a very important source of memory and understanding for him.[12] "Much of my writing still reflects the cadences of the language in the scriptures. A lot of my sentences begin with conjunctions (for example, 'and' and 'but') the way Joseph Smith's sentences did."[13]

When he was six years old, he gave his first talk in church, which he wrote himself and memorized. "That was also about the age I sang my first duet, with a little girl from the ward [congregation]. But that's how it is in the Mormon church—kids pray and speak and recite and sing from the start."[14]

Not surprisingly, Scott did well in school. In Grades 4 and 5 he was part of a group of children who took part in special "gifted" sessions. There he was taught Spanish and other useful subjects.

Among his favorite classes were music classes. He started with the clarinet because his parents already owned one—his brother had given it a try. But he did not really like playing the clarinet, so when his parents asked him if he wanted to continue playing it, he said no, and they sold it. The next year, though, the band teacher wanted him back in the band, and suggested he take up the French horn instead—both because the band teacher needed a French horn player and because the school could lend Scott the instrument. Scott would play the French horn until his last year of high school; he also played tuba or sousaphone (in fact, in high school, he made the Arizona All-Star Band as a sousaphone player).[15]

He also sang—a lot. When the family took road trips, they would sing in the car. Among other things, they sang songs by the great musical theater composers and lyricists: Rodgers and Hammerstein, Lerner and Loewe, Cole Porter, the Gerswhins, Rodgers and Hart. Scott and his mother particularly loved to sing duets. "I had a knack for harmony—I'd make it up as I went along, even at the age of seven or eight."[16]

Driving, Card remembers, was one of his father's pleasures. So were photography, model planes that really flew, and "all kinds of gadgets." His father wrote scripts for presentations, painted signs, and painted pictures. "He did a wire-and-string project for an art class that occupied a place of pride in our living room," Card says. "I took it for granted that people in our family did art that was good enough for public consumption."[17]

At church, Scott's father was a good interpreter of scripture. He taught his son that there were legitimate interpretations of scripture, and then there were "wacko ideas" that needed to be corrected because they were out of line with scripture. He explained that it was important not just to have "feeling" about religion, but also a sound understanding of it. "He was the one who intercepted my learning about cavemen at school and told me about contrary ideas of creation in the Mormon Church," Card recalls. His father taught him that it is possible to hold two contradictory ideas in your mind at the same time, without having to decide at once—and for all time—which is right. As his father put it, "Just remember, whenever religion and science disagree, one or the other or both of them will eventually change."[18]

Scott's mother was a performer, a trained singer and also an excellent actress and director. "She and my Dad would write road shows—fifteen minute plays that were entered into annual competitions at church, with funny new lyrics to existing songs."[19]

That may have been why Scott's father had an occasional subscription to *Writer's Digest* magazine and talked about story ideas sometimes. Certainly Scott did not think there was anything unusual or difficult about writing. He had grandparents who were poets and lyricists. His mother had written the script for a musical called *The*

*Bradford Girls* that was produced in Richland, Washington, about the time she was pregnant with Scott. (It featured songs with lyrics by his grandmother and music by his uncle Gordon, his mother's oldest brother.) His father also wrote and created multimedia presentations for San Jose State and Lockheed.[20]

And so, it was natural that at some point Scott would try his hand at writing.

At about age ten, Scott wrote a story about a smart kid who was beaten by bullies and became brain-damaged and retarded. He was inspired partly by his own run-in with the bully at the bridge when he was six, and partly by a story his mother told him about a smart kid who was beaten up by bullies to the point of brain damage when she was in school. His mother submitted it to a couple of magazines, but it was not accepted.[21]

That did not bother Scott; he was not setting out on a career as a writer at that young age. He did not really see writing a story as a big deal. "Writing was normal in my family," Card says. "It was just something you did."[22]

Scott himself had moved beyond his early fear of bullies by learning to talk his way out of trouble. When threatened, he would simply agree that, "Yes, you can beat me up, I'm weak and slow and I don't know how to fight, so big deal, beating me up would be easy. All it proves is that you don't actually have any answer for what I said. So beating me up is just another way of admitting I'm right."

That did not always work, and he did have to occasionally worry about some threatened after school encounter, but none of the bullies ever followed through. "I think ultimately they realized my answer was correct—or their friends pointed it out to them, that it would just make them look mean and stupid to fight me."[23]

Besides, Card says, "My school didn't *have* that many bullies."[24]

But he would soon be changing schools. The family had expanded by two while in Santa Clara: Delpha Elizabeth was born in March 1958, and Arlen Lester was born in April 1961. And in 1964, when Scott was thirteen, the Card clan moved to Mesa, Arizona.

Chapter 4

# BYU to Brazil and Back

Willard Card had been laid off by Lockheed some months earlier. That gave him the impetus to get back to what he really wanted to do—teach. He landed a job as assistant professor at Arizona State University in Tempe. However, he moved his family to Mesa rather than Tempe because at the time Mesa, which had been founded by Mormons, was about 50 percent Mormon.[1]

Changing schools is never easy, but the move to Mesa was not as hard on Scott as it might have been. "I quickly found the smart kids, plus being in the band gives you instant friends—at least if you get made first chair on your first day there."[2]

Scott also fit in easily because, for the first time, Mormons were not in a minority in his school. "I was used to being the only Mormon in my class, so it was a relief to be able to talk religion," he says. "Plus, there were a couple of Baptist teachers at the school whose project was to lure Mormon kids away from their faith, and I became the champion at answering their arguments, until they banned me from their anti-Mormon afterschool sessions, whereupon I complained about them to the administration and the sessions stopped."

He suspects his parents had something to do with that, since his mother worked for the school district at the time and might have spoken to the principal. Nevertheless, he says, "being a champion pro-Mormon arguer didn't lose me any friends."[3]

But it was another of Scott's passions, politics, that really made him "famous." Scott had been interested in politics since listening to his parents discuss the presidential campaign of 1960, in which Republican Richard Nixon ran against Democrat John F. Kennedy. They did not like either candidate, but ended up voting for Nixon. "They claimed to be independents, but I never heard of them voting for anyone but a Republican, ever. Still, there was no pressure. I made up my own mind."[4]

Four years later, when Scott was in Mesa, the presidential campaign was between Republican—and Arizonan—Barry Goldwater and Democrat Lyndon B. Johnson. The school decided to hold a mock presidential debate in a school assembly, but could not find anyone to represent the pro-Johnson side.

"Even though I was pro-Goldwater at the time, and everyone knew it, I volunteered to argue the Johnson side and did a good job of it," Card says. "In fact, I remember being frustrated that the pro-Goldwater people couldn't figure out how to answer some of my points—I knew how to answer me! But it wasn't my job to coach them."[5] A couple of kids actually got angry with him, convinced he must really be a Democrat.

"After that, there wasn't anybody at school who didn't know who Scott Card was," Card says. "My time in Mesa was the period of my life when I had the most friends and was at my most socially successful. . . . Odd, because eighth to tenth grades are usually social death for smart kids who don't dress 'cool' and have no athletic ability."[6]

Even though one reason Scott was popular in the Mesa school was because he could effectively make pro-Mormon arguments, by the time he was twelve he was finding that the church programs no longer fit his interests. The main activity provided for boys his age was the Boy Scouts. "I went on campouts," he says, "but hated the food, hated the tents, hated the bugs, and hated the boys. Even the boys I liked became mean and aggressive and competitive while on a campout, and scornful of my lack of skill and interest in what was going on."[7]

Scott did not hate the outdoors—he loved wandering through the woods. He just did not like doing it as part of an organized group, or being forced to do things more dangerous or uncomfortable than he would have chosen for himself. "I didn't like the macho attitude of the leaders. And nobody would just let me sit in the shade and read, which to my mind was what the woods were for."[8]

Things did not improve, church-program-wise, as Scott grew older. In fact, they got worse. The emphasis shifted to "endless series of career-day-type trips and basketball games."[9] Although Scott liked basketball, he was not very good at it, and the games as played did not provide him with an opportunity to get any better. "They were always playing for blood and got angry and hateful when I [messed] up. How could I get better, when they—and I—didn't want me to play at all?"[10]

Scott liked physical activity, but not team sports. Instead, he preferred solitary things like hiking and climbing. He loved wandering through the Arizona desert. "Though I could get as lonely as anyone, I was profoundly introverted and loved my solitary time."[11]

His dislike of organized sports extended to the organized sports in high school. "What I truly hated was the viciousness of boys playing sports. The utter lack of team spirit, the cruel disregard for the pride of less-talented players. Every now and then someone showed patience enough to teach me something, but that was far overshadowed by the cruel jeers directed, sometimes toward me, but always toward *someone*.

"I also hated football because I loathed physical contact and dreaded being hurt," he adds. He was first drawn to basketball because he thought it was a noncontact sport, but "when the elbows started flying, I was out forever."[12]

Worse than organized sports themselves was the way athletes were the object of adulation, whereas those who were good at the things school was supposedly for—i.e., academics—were despised. As an A student, Scott was one of the latter.

In his sophomore year in Mesa, he decided to do something about it. "I calculatedly started openly scorning football players, mocking them in clever-but-cruel ways in the halls at school. Naturally, they could have beaten me up—but as I said, I was clever. I always scorned them in ways that were vague enough that they'd look really stupid if they took offense openly. But me and my group of intellectual friends became one of the dominant social groups. Proto-nerd jokes either rolled off my back or got such devastating replies that they soon stopped."[13]

One of his "intellectual friends" was his closest friend in high school, Sam Cristler. He was not a Mormon; he was a Southern Baptist. "We'd argue religion for hours, but always in a way that left us friends during and after the discussion," Card says. "True civil conversation."[14]

Forced to look at his own religion through an outsider's eyes, Scott came to understand things about it that probably would not have come up if he had only looked at it from the inside. Neither friend converted the other, nor were they trying to.

What mattered was that they understood each other's faith.

But even while Scott was arguing religion with his best friend, he was becoming more and more disillusioned with his own church—not with its doctrine, but with its programs.

His favorite church activities were the road shows, dance festivals, and speech festivals that were an important part of the Mormon tradition. "I excelled at those things, loved doing them, and, best of all, even when there was a competition, nobody was competitive—nobody got angry or swore or cheated in order to win, the way they did in basketball. If you weren't as good, people helped you until you were, instead of insisting you warm the bench while they did it right.

"So naturally, the church soon completely abandoned the drama, speech and dance programs—and kept scouting and basketball. It's as if they decided they weren't interested in holding on to young men like me. Drove me crazy."[15]

The result was that by the age of sixteen, Scott had essentially dropped out of the church's program for young men. He kept going to Sunday School but found that he knew more about the scriptures than his teachers did, and more about church doctrine, too. When they taught something false or inaccurate, he would try, "as nicely as I knew how, which wasn't very," to set them straight. For his pains, he was called before a bishop and told to stop causing trouble for teachers. The bishop agreed that Scott's understanding of the issues was correct, but when Scott then asked if he was expected to let the teacher teach false doctrine, the bishop told him he had a bad and defiant attitude.

"And this was in the sixties," Card says. "I thought: I could be taking drugs, drinking, sleeping around, dressing like a hippie, wearing my hair long, all kinds of things—but what you want to chew me out over is that I'm insisting that the teacher teach the gospel correctly."[16]

**"I excelled at those things [drama, speech, and dance]."**

**—Orson Scott Card**

So he dropped out of Sunday School. He continued going to what his parents called the "commanded meetings"—in the Mormon church, the Sacrament Meeting and the Priesthood Meeting—and performing his duties, but even there he was unhappy, disgusted with the other young men, who he felt had no understanding of what they were doing, and disgusted with the leadership, who would choose the boys he thought were the least spiritual—though most popular—as quorum leaders.

"Fortunately," Card says, "at that point I got out of high school a year early and went to BYU [Brigham Young University]."[17]

In fact, the entire family went to BYU—or,

more precisely, to Orem, Utah—because Willard Card had gotten a job at the university in nearby Provo. Although it was not a faculty position [it was on the educational media staff] it did offer a chance to teach a couple of classes. It was not long before he became a full-time faculty member. Peggy Card, meanwhile, got a job at Utah Fish & Game.

The family moved in 1967, at the end of Scott's sophomore year in high school. He officially had two years left, but even in Mesa his parents were discussing the possibility of getting him to college early. In Utah, he was able to attend an individual-progress school and finish high school early, receiving his diploma at the end of what would have been his junior year.[18] The school also allowed students to take individual college classes while still in high school, something Scott did.[19]

His parents were excited by the move. It had been their dream and plan all along to eventually return to Utah. Scott was excited, too. Utah was where they went to visit relatives—grandparents and some cousins—and BYU was the school where his older sister had gone to college and where he had always expected to go. And Utah, of course was "the center of the universe for Mormons."[20]

The family lived in a three-bedroom two-bathroom ranch-style house at 370 South 650 East. The house had a full unfinished basement, which Willard Card subdivided into rooms. For the first time in his life, Scott had a room of his own. So did all of his brothers and sisters. "Maybe that's why I didn't resist going," Card says. "He promised that to me right from the start and that sounded like heaven . . . and on top of that, I got to help him build the partitions. My dad was a real do-it-yourselfer and I loved working with him on cool projects—at least the ones that could be finished in a couple of hours."[21]

At first Scott wanted to major in archaeology. He was drawn to it because of the fledgling field of Mormon archaeology, and because he had read about the exciting work of men like Thor Heyerdahl.[22] (Heyerdahl undertook a number of spectacular expeditions; he was probably most famous for building a balsawood raft, *Kon-Tiki*, and sailing it 4,300 miles from Peru to the Polynesian island of Raroia, in support of his theory that the islands were settled from South America.)[23]

Card was soon disillusioned with archaeology, however—not the state of the science, but the fact that doing the research he was interested in would mean "a lot of hard work in hot climates."[24]

Since he had gravitated to the theater department and was already spending all his time there, he decided to switch his major to theater in the fall semester of his freshman year. "I figured that whatever I loved doing, I'd be good at, and that would be my career."[25]

At first he focused on acting, but although he was not terrible at it, he also was not one of the best. Instead, he learned everything else that went into putting on plays: set design, construction, makeup, costuming, directing—everything except lighting. "Bad acrophobia [fear of heights]," he explains. "I simply couldn't go up and aim the lights."[26]

He also learned directing, and it was through directing that he found the aspect of theater that he loved the most: playwriting.

He was assistant director of a production of *Flowers for Algernon*. "It had a terrible second act, so I asked the director for permission to try my hand at rewriting it, based on the original story and novel. He let me give it a try, and ended up using my version. And it worked on stage."[27]

Next, for another class, he created a half-read, half-acted version of *Tell Me That You Love Me, Junie Moon*, and directed a production of it, "using some extraordinarily talented actors." It was a hit, thanks to word-of-mouth. They had a packed house the second—and final—night. "People laughed all the way through it and sobbed at the end," Card says. "Contrast that with the lame movie made from the book, and my script won hands down."[28]

After that, Card began trying to write his own original plays, and quickly discovered that was something quite different, since the story had to be created from scratch. He also found that it was hard to create a script that would hold together over multiple acts—and that "if you have enough scenes that work, the audience doesn't notice that the overall play didn't have a good structure."[29]

He was also spurred to write plays based on

Mormon scripture and history. Some bad ones, in his view, were already beginning to appear in the Mormon community. "I knew I could do better—and I did."[30]

His dedication to the gospel had suddenly found a useful and appreciated outlet. "When I wrote plays about Mormon subjects, suddenly I was a hero—whereas my study of the gospel had made me a pariah in my home ward. Ironic, eh?" BYU, he says, was like "being at a really good church meeting every day."[31]

In all, Scott wrote more than a dozen full-length plays and several one-act plays at BYU. Things were going great, and Scott was within a year of completing his bachelor's degree in theater, when he shocked his family by applying to serve a mission.

Mormon young men are eligible to serve as missionaries for two years at the age of nineteen if they are "worthy." (You are worthy if you are a commandment-keeping member of the church, which means sexual chastity; no alcohol, smoking or drugs, not even coffee or tea; tithing—giving 10 percent of annual income to the church—; and attending church.)

"I had no problems on any of those points," Card says, but when he had turned nineteen he had been busy and uninterested in going. It was only a year later, when everyone else had given up on his serving, that he felt, as he puts it, "a kind of emptiness. I knew I was missing something. There was a vague sense that if I didn't serve a mission, I wouldn't be the man I wanted to be—the father my children would need."[32]

And so he applied. The destination was up to the church leadership. Scott dreaded the possibility of being sent to Korea or Japan because he did not think he could stand the food. Fortunately for his digestion, he was sent to Brazil, which delighted him; he had even studied Portugese in high school.

Card will not provide a lot of detail about his time in Brazil. "It's either a book in itself, or nothing, I'm afraid," he says. "Let's just say that I emerged fifty pounds lighter—more from exercise than picky eating—with a healthy respect for the top leadership of the church and a withering contempt for a certain kind of salesmanship attitude that is too frequent among mission presidents." His first mission president was terrible, he says; his second was good, and he learned a lot from both of them. Perhaps more important from the point of view of his future writing, "I also learned a lot about human nature from the behavior of other missionaries and from the many local Church members and investigators (people studying the gospel) I came to know. I ended up loving Brazil—the people, the country, the language; and with a stronger and wiser and way less naïve view of the way the church works and what it does for the people who believe in it." He also came back with a new play, *Stone Tables*, about Moses and the Exodus, which he wrote partly because he missed using the English language.[33]

His high-school talks with his friend Sam

Cristler played an important role in preparing him for his mission, Card says; so did his home life when he was growing up. Not only his parents' example of dedicated service to God, but also the fact that they talked about their faith: philosophically, historically, and personally.

"Both my parents, with different styles, taught us important things. I also read the scriptures from an early age, with the encouragement of my parents, and they were knowledgeable enough to discuss anything and everything with me. No matter what road I went down in my childhood, they had already been there. They also kept a house full of important books. . . . In a way, I grew up in a theological seminary . . . where they made me go out and weed the lawn."[34]

Scott returned from his mission in 1973 and finished his bachelor's degree in theater with distinction in 1975.

A whole new adventure beckoned.

## Chapter 5

# First Sale and Marriage

Card fully expected to pursue a life in the theater, and even before receiving his degree began working toward establishing his own theater company. "I had dreams of establishing a Mormon repertory theater company," he says. "Shakespeare was my model—I wanted a company like the one he wrote for and acted in."[1]

Established in 1974, the Utah Valley Repertory Theatre Company ran for two summer seasons and one fall-spring season. Card had dreams of the company doing so well it would one day be able to build its own theater and of producing primarily Mormon plays. There were not enough Mormon scripts to start with, though, and the theater needed to build an audience, so the first summer season featured a variety of plays and musicals, including two that Card directed himself: *Camelot* and *Romeo and Juliet*.

Both were well-suited to the venue, a theater called the Castle that had been built during the Depression with federal funds but had never been used because its location, behind the state mental hospital in Provo, just was not convenient. (Convenient or not, it had one very important thing going for it: the mental hospital let the theater company use it rent-free.)

"It was an exhilarating experience as my friends and I created theater to a very high standard . . . and built an audience," Card says, adding that he's seen much worse off-Broadway—and on. "We had good audiences and, with competent business management (which we did not have, since it was me) we would have eventually made it work."[2]

But despite no rent to pay, unpaid actors, props and costume materials donated by cast members and other acts of "incredible generosity" (the family of one company member, Jon Swindle, even lent the company a van to transport those unable to manage the walk up the steep climb from the parking lot to the Castle), that first summer season ended with the company—that is, Card—$600 in debt, thanks to unavoidable expenses like royalties, lights, and so on.[3]

"I knew it was time to get a real job," Card says. He heard that BYU Press needed part-time proofreaders, and he applied. Between his experience proofreading the dissertations his mother typed when he was growing up, and his own solid knowledge of English grammar and spelling, he got the job. He quickly learned a lot about editing as well as proofreading. He applied for the first opening as a copy editor (a full-time job), and got that as well. In a relatively short time he moved up to an editor's job.[4]

In the meantime, he had decided that the Utah Valley Theatre Repertory Company would go ahead with a fall season, which proved to be a "disaster."

He got two investors to cosign a loan, "which they regretted almost immediately," to convert an old barn in Provo into a theater and build sets. He wrote his own adaptation of *A Christmas Carol*, which worked very well, but a Halloween production of *Dracula*, adapted by another director, "barely had any attendance at all."

The company continued into the spring—one of the productions was of another Card script, *Liberty Jail*, based on Mormon history—but all in all, the experience in the barn, Card says, "was absolutely dreadful." Both Card and the barn's owner lost money.

The company returned to the Castle in the summer of 1975, when an over-budget production of *King Lear* became the straw that broke the company's back. "At that point, with my pathetic income from BYU Press and a huge load of debt [$20,000][5] from the remodeling of the barn, I called it quits and set to work to try to make money as a fiction writer in order to repay the losses."[6]

And so, Card dusted off his short story "The Tinker," sent it to *Analog*, and when that was rejected, wrote a "real" science fiction story, "Ender's Game," which editor Ben Bova accepted.

"Ender's Game" marked the real start of Card's career as a fiction writer. But although he was elated by the sale, he says he was "not so stupid as to quit my job."[7]

At the time he wrote "Ender's Game," in 1974, he was working at BYU Press. By the time it was published, in August 1977, he had long since changed jobs. In 1975 he became a full-time assistant editor at *The Ensign*, the official magazine of the Church of Jesus Christ of Latter-day Saints, which necessitated a move from Provo to Salt Lake City. Card worked at *The Ensign* through 1977.

Card says being an *Ensign* editor taught him a lot about structure in writing, because he had to take other people's articles and essays apart and recast them to meet the magazine's needs. He also met regularly for lunch with two other *Ensign* editors, Jay Parry and Lane Johnson, who were also aspiring fiction writers. The three would discuss story ideas in the cafeteria downstairs in the LDS's Church Office Building at 50 East North Temple, and some of the ideas that emerged in later Card stories took shape there.

In addition to rewriting other writers' submissions, Card got the opportunity to write original pieces. In July 1977 *The Ensign* put out a Fine Arts issue. Card wrote three pieces for it: an essay on including the arts in child-rearing, a play (published under the pseudonym "Brian Green"), and a short story called "Gert Fram"—which came out just before the August 1977 issue of *Analog* with "Ender's Game" in it, making "Gert Fram" Card's first published story.

But it was "Ender's Game" that launched Card's writing career. As Michael A. Collings puts it in the introduction to *Storyteller: The Official Orson Scott Card Bibliography*, it "almost by itself established Card as an important new voice in science fiction . . . the story first told in skeleton form in that original version continues to entrance and engage readers."[8]

Something else very important happened in those years between the end of Card's mission in Brazil and the career-launching publication of "Ender's Game": Card got married.

Card first got to know Kristine Allen when she was in a road show he directed before his mission (just before—it was not actually performed until after he had left). She wrote him toward the end of his mission, and, he says, "she was my first date after I came home."[9]

While he had been gone, she had been very active with a drama program Card's mother ran in their ward. As a result, her family and the Card family had become close. "She actually started writing to me to make sure that when I came home, I didn't ruin everything," Card jokes.[10]

He bought a diamond that he intended to give her as a surprise his first Christmas home, in 1974. ("With a plan of letting her choose her own setting; I thought it was insane for guys to actually buy the whole ring as a surprise!")[11]

But the path of true love does not necessarily run smoothly, and with two breakups in between, Card and Kristine did not become engaged for another two years, until just before New Year's 1977.[12]

They were married on May 17, 1977, at the Temple in Salt Lake City, with Elder LeGrand Richards of the LDS Quorum of the Twelve Apostles officiating and Card's and Kristine's fathers as legal witnesses.

In a way, Card's career as a novelist and his life as a married man began on the same day: he mailed off the manuscript for his first novel, *Hot Sleep*, that morning in the LDS Church Office Building, then took the tunnel under the street that connected the office building to the temple.[13]

In the process, he introduced Kristine to life with a freelance writer. Copying, packaging, and mailing the manuscript took longer than he expected, so he showed up a few minutes late for the signing-in that occurred before the bride and groom got dressed for the ceremony—causing Kristine a moment of worry.

But "the wedding ceremony went off precisely on time," Card hastens to add. "I wouldn't want people to think of her standing at the altar looking at her watch. I'm not *that* irresponsible."[14]

Orson Scott Card's writing career truly began with the short story "Ender's Game," which he wrote in 1974.

As 1977 wound down, Card believed that he could support himself and a family through free-lance writing alone. His first book had been published (a nonfiction discussion of child-rearing called *"Listen, Mom and Dad . . . ": Young Adults Look Back on Their Upbringing*, published by Bookcraft in Salt Lake City). He had also sold two novels by then (although the advances for both books combined were only slightly more than half of what he earned as an editor for *The Ensign*), and additional short stories, both science fiction stories and children's stories for a Mormon audience.

In addition, he had begun to write audio dramatizations for a company called Living Scriptures in Ogden, Utah, earning about $100 for each half-hour script. "At first I was writing about LDS Church history, and I relied heavily on narration to make up for the lack of visuals. But as I learned what could be accomplished through sound effects and suggestion, I eventually got to where I never used a narrator at all—it was a point of pride," Card says. "I wrote for them until the mid 1980s."[15]

In the fall of 1977 Card took a three-week leave of absence from *The Ensign* to prove to Kristine (and himself) that he could produce work steadily enough to pay the rent and the bills. "She needed the proof, because she was pregnant with Geoffrey by then, and she got such violent morning sickness she could not stay at her job," Card recalls. "I did well enough that she never went back to employment—except to manage our own financial affairs." Beginning in 1978, Card became a full-time freelance writer, and never regretted the decision. "I never had a year as a freelancer in which I earned less than twice as much as I would have gotten at *The Ensign*," he says.[16]

"Ender's Game," in the August 1977 issue of *Analog* marked Card's science fiction debut. A series of additional stories over the next few months, all bought by *Analog* editor Ben Bova, cemented Card's position as a writer to watch. "Malpractice" appeared in the November 1977 *Analog* and "Follower" in the February 1978 issue; "Kingsmeat" in the anthology, *Analog* Yearbook, in March 1978; "Happy Head" in the April 1978 *Analog*, "Mikal's Songbird" in the May issue, and "I Put My Blue Genes On" in the August issue.[17]

Readers took note. One of the major awards in the science fiction field is the John W. Campbell Award for Best New Writer, sponsored by *Analog*. In 1978, that award went to Orson Scott Card.

In addition, "Ender's Game" placed second on the ballot for the 1978 Hugo Award for Best Short Story, and was also recommended for (although it did not make the final ballot) the 1978 Nebula Award for Best Short Story.

"The John W. Campbell Award was nice, but the Hugo would have been nicer," Card says. However, "the Campbell Award made foreign publishers notice me, and since my agent, Barbara Bova, was smart enough to hold on to 100 percent

## The Hugos and the Nebulas[18]

The Hugo Awards, distinctive rocketship-shaped trophies, are the top awards of the science fiction field. They have been given annually since 1953, and now include more than a dozen categories, including best books, stories, dramatic works, and professional and fan activities. They are nominated for and voted on by members of the annual World Science Fiction Convention, representing the field's most committed fans and professionals.

The Nebula Awards are comparable to the Oscars: they are presented by professionals to professionals. They were created in 1966 by the newly formed Science Fiction Writers of America, originally as the basis for annual anthologies that could provide income to the organization.

of my foreign rights, that made a big financial difference. Almost as soon as she became my agent, my income doubled because of foreign sales, which for many years were about equal to my American fiction income."[19]

Card says he did not feel any pressure to "live up" to that—or subsequent—awards. "There's only pressure to come up with really good stories that I and, hopefully, my readers will enjoy, and then write a manuscript that deals with all the problems and tells the story effectively."[20]

In January 1979, Card's career took another step forward with the publication by Ace of his first fiction book, *Capitol*, a collection of related short stories, some previously published, others written just for that book. The stories are all set in a futuristic society built around a drug called *somec*, which puts recipients into suspended animation (so they can survive the decades-long journeys between stars) but robs them of their memories. However, technology allows memories to be recorded and played back once the person awakens.

Three months later, Card's first novel, *Hot Sleep*—the one he mailed the morning of his wedding—was published by Baronet in trade paperback, with a mass-market paperback following the next month from Ace. (Mass-market paperbacks are what most people think of as paperbacks: they are small, usually printed on lower-quality paper, and sold both in and outside of bookstores, in places like drugstores and airport newsstands. Trade paperbacks are typically larger, use higher-quality paper, and are intended for sale in bookstores.) By the end of the year, his second novel, *A Planet Called Treason*, had come out in hardcover from St. Martin's.

Reviews were mixed. Bradley Sinor, writing in *Science Fiction and Fantasy Book Review*, thought the story cycle in *Capitol* "did not hang together very well," but called Card "a skilled craftsman and a writer to watch."[21] *Publisher's Weekly* thought the stories demonstrated "a fine talent for storytelling and characterization, if a rather dour outlook."[22]

*Hot Sleep* is set in the same universe as the stories in *Capitol*—they are all part of *The Worthing Chronicle*, as was "Tinker," the short story Card wrote before his mission. In *Science Fiction and Fantasy Book Review*, Fred Niederman called *Hot Sleep* "fresh, intelligent and interesting,"[23] but in the *Magazine of Fantasy and Science Fiction*, Michael Bishop called it "a weird, as well as bad book."[24]

**"My first novel was published despite its flaws."**

**—Orson Scott Card**

*A Planet Called Treason* attracted not just mixed reviews, but controversy—something Card has been no stranger to over the ensuing years. Reviewers in *Publisher's Weekly* and *Analog* were enthusiastic. Others were not. In particular, Mormon critic Sandra Straubhaar attacked the novel for gratuitous violence and sexism, and failing to propagate the Mormon faith.[25]

Card thinks critics like Straubhaar misunderstood the book, but he has his own problems with both of his first two novels, noting that they were "amateurish in some of the choices I made."

"My first novel was published despite its flaws," he says of *Hot Sleep*. "I was glad to have the chance to rewrite it and publish it again" (in 1983 as *The Worthing Chronicle*). "My second novel I also wanted to rewrite completely, but the publisher of that book refused to give me time. Even at that, I still rewrote the beginning completely and did some substantial editing in order to bring *A Planet Called Treason* out as *Treason* ten years later."[26] (*Treason* was published in hardcover by St. Martin's Press in 1988). *Hot Sleep* and *A Planet Called Treason* remain the only published novels Card has ever rewritten.

One of the odd things about writing books is that it can be months or years before they appear in print. "By the time *Capitol* came out, I was already hard at work on *Songmaster* (the novel that would follow *A Planet Called Treason*)," Card points out. "*Capitol* was already old news. It was fun to hold the book, but . . . like an award, it lasted about ten minutes before the thrill was gone and it was just another book on the shelf. Albeit the first fiction entry on a shelf of my books, in which I take some pride."[27]

Besides, Card and his wife had a much greater, ongoing thrill to enjoy: their first son, Michael Geoffrey, was born on April 25, 1978.[28]

"A book was nothing compared to our first baby," Card says. "I mean, the book is there, but it doesn't change. Babies change all the time. Endlessly fascinating. And unlike my novels, I don't know how they're going to turn out."[29]

## Chapter 6

# Children and Challenges

At first, after leaving *The Ensign*, Card continued to do quite a bit of freelance editing as well as writing, but that soon changed. "Gradually the freelance editing faded as I priced myself out of the market (deliberately) and my writing of books and audio scripts brought in more money than editing ever could," he says.[1]

Freelancing also meant the freedom to live somewhere other than Salt Lake City. After the birth of Michael Geoffrey, the Cards wanted to live closer to family, and they were ready to buy a house,[2] so in 1979 they moved: first to Sandy, Utah, and then to Orem, so Kristine could be close to her family while Card could pursue a master's degree in English at the University of Utah.[3] At about the same time, his next novel, *Songmaster*, appeared from Dial Books.

*Songmaster* grew out of the novelette "Mikal's Songbird," which appeared in the May 1978 issue of *Analog*. A finalist for the Nebula Award in 1978 and the Hugo Award in 1979, "Mikal's Songbird" would probably have stayed a novelette if not for the urging of his agent, Barbara Bova. She phoned Card and told him she had just received a pretty good offer from a publisher for a novel version of "Mikal's Songbird." Card was not at all sure he could turn it into a novel—as far as he was concerned, it was finished. Nevertheless, after some deliberation, he came up with an idea that intrigued him. It also gave him an approach to turning a shorter work into a longer one that he's used many times since: "The place to go for new material isn't after the initial short story, but before it," he explains. "By starting much earlier, and explaining how the characters got to where they are at the beginning of the short story, the milieu is much richer, the cast of characters much fuller, the characterization much deeper than it was in the original story."[4]

"Much outlining and map-drawing later," he began writing. The first section was published as a stand-alone novella by Stanley Schmidt, who had taken over as editor of *Analog* from Ben Bova. The finished book, Card notes, had hardly a word of "Mikal's Songbird" left in it: "Events had new meanings; characters had different things to think and say."

In hindsight, Card thinks *Songmaster* has some structural flaws. He puts those down to his relative unfamiliarity with writing novels at that early point in his career, not the fact it was expanded from a short story. Despite those problems, he says, "*Songmaster* is my earliest novel that I am willing to stand by in its original form. . . . The structure has problems, but I'm willing to live with them, because the story still feels true to me as it stands, even if it isn't as artful as I'd like."[5]

Card considers *Songmaster* important to his development as a writer. He notes that the original novelette, "Mikal's Songbird," came at a crucial time in his career. "Ender's Game" had been his first science fiction sale, and he had found it easy to write. But his next story "died instantly," and although his third and fourth sold to *Analog*, they were only made publishable thanks to strong editorial guidance from Ben Bova.

"The next few stories I wrote, however, went nowhere—they were so bad that not only did no one buy them, but also one editor sent me an incredible two-page letter that can only be classed as hate-mail. . . . These stories were so bad that someone had to drive a stake through their hearts, just to make sure they didn't rise again."

And after those debacles, Card says, "I was afraid. . . . I had no guarantee that I'd have a career in a genre that actually paid writers enough to live on. To me, at that bleak moment, it looked as though 'Ender's Game' might be the only successful story I'd ever write."

For his next attempt, therefore, he went back to "Ender's Game" and analyzed it. He decided to create a story that followed roughly the same pattern—a child with extraordinary ability goes through a great deal of personal pain inflicted by adults trying to exploit him. (In "Mikal's Songbird," the extraordinary ability was musical, not military-related.)

Card wrote the story quickly and mailed it "still hot from Xeroxing" to Ben Bova. Then he reread it, and realized it had serious flaws. He quickly rewrote it, and sent the revised version to *Analog*, with a note to the effect that Bova should ignore the previous version. As it happened, Bova had already decided to buy the first version. (Of course, in the end, the revised version was the one printed.)

It was upon getting the check from Bova for the first version of "Mikal's Songbird," Card says, that "I knew I had a career—not because I had found a repeatable formula, for in fact I had not, but rather because I had found a road into that place inside myself from which true stories arise."[6]

From the start of the development of *Songmaster*, then, the story was continuously derived from previous versions. As a result, Card says, "Every version represents another stage in my self-schooling as a writer of narrative."

That includes the novel version. "I knew that *Hot Sleep* was a failure as a novel. . . . I was also beginning to realize that *A Planet Called Treason* was rushed, sketchy, abrupt, not a smoothly flowing work. In other words, I still didn't know how to write a novel."

He tried to train himself by carefully examining Saul Bellow's novel *Humboldt's Gift*. By doing so, he says, he felt he gained a feel for a novel's pace, so that when he sat down to work on *Songmaster*, he was able to keep that same rhythm of "event, language and scene."

**"I still didn't know how to write a novel."**

**—Orson Scott Card**

"As a result," he says, "*Songmaster* was my one story with explicit connections with other works, a clear pattern of growth and change that paralleled my own. Expanding it to a novel may have come from a commercially minded editor's suggestion to my agent, and my own source for the story's idea may have been a deliberate mining of my own previous work, but it ended up as a story I believed in passionately—and the process of writing it was a kind of training ground for my career as a writer, just as my characters Ender and Ansset (the main character in *Songmaster*) had to go through training to become a person capable of surviving."[7]

By the time *Songmaster* appeared in print, nearly forty Orson Scott Card stories had appeared, along with six books, many poems, and many nonfiction pieces.[8] His freelance writing career seemed secure.

And Card never doubted that it was his career—but he also had what he now calls a "hobby": the pursuit of higher education.[9] He obtained his master's degree from the University of Utah in 1981, and in the summer of that year Card and his growing family (he and Kristine had their second child, Emily Janice, on August 17, 1980) moved to South Bend, Indiana, so Card could work toward a Ph.D. at Notre Dame University.

"We looked out of state for a university (I was also accepted at Duke) for my doctorate—we wanted an out-of-Utah degree specifically so we could be hired at a Utah university when I had a

---

## Of the naming of children

All of Orson Scott Card's children were given at least one name in honor of a writer that he and his wife admired. Thus:

Michael Geoffrey (for Geoffrey Chaucer)

Emily Janice (for Emily Bronte and Emily Dickinson)

Charles Benjamin (for Charles Dickens)

Zina Margaret (for Margaret Mitchell)

Erin Louisa (for Louisa May Alcott).[10]

---

degree. We applied to schools east of the Mississippi so that our kids would have the experience of living, for a time, in a diverse culture, and because I wanted to get out of the desert.

"I never expected to choose between academia and writing. I was already supporting my family by writing and expected to continue to do so. I intended to teach in my spare time, the way I was getting my Ph.D. (and got my M.A.)."[11]

Card taught freshman composition at both the University of Utah and at Notre Dame. At the University of Utah he was forbidden to assign readings to his composition students ("which was ridiculous," he says[12]), but at the University of Notre Dame the composition course included a literature component, which the teachers could design themselves.

Card made eclectic choices: he would have the students read and analyze Robert Cormier's young adult classic *I Am the Cheese*, then have them read *King Lear* by William Shakespeare—first ordering them to avoid all commentaries and notes on the play and to concentrate solely on the text.[13]

But before Card received his Ph.D., the economy intervened and changed his plans.

By 1983, Card had written or edited eleven books. In the science fiction genre, *Songmaster* had been followed by the short-story collection *Unaccompanied Sonata and Other Stories; Hart's Hope* in early January 1983; and *The Worthing Chronicle*, the rewritten version of *Hot Sleep*, in July of that year. He had also edited *Dragons of*

*Light* and *Dragons of Darkness*, two anthologies of dragon-related fiction and art.

In 1982, he had also had two nonfiction books published, *Saintspeak: The Mormon Dictionary*, a humorous satirical dictionary of Christian and Mormon terms, and *Ainge*, a biography of Brigham Young University basketball star Danny Ainge.

But "they were holding a recession in the early '80s," Card says. As a result, "publishers stopped buying books—at least from writers at my level at the time. They had a two-year backlog, so why borrow money at such high interest rates?"[14]

Card also says that his publisher at the time, Berkley, had lost faith in him as a writer. His next book for Berkley was to be *Saints* (published in 1984 under the title *A Woman of Destiny*, but republished under its original title in 1988). It was an in-depth historical novel of the early Mormon era (specifically the church's 19th-century practice of polygamy). "By following *their* editorial direction on *Saints*, I had ended up with a book that the book clubs didn't want," Card says. "I warned them; they didn't listen; but when it went south, it was *my* fault."[15]

With no new book offers forthcoming, a salary insufficient without additional freelance income to support his family, and a third child on the way, Card began looking for a job. He was offered two: one in Hartford, Connecticut, with the videogame company Coleco, and one in Greensboro, North Carolina, with *Compute!* Books.[16] He took the latter, and early in 1983, the Card family moved to Greensboro.

The next nine months proved difficult. They would eventually find their way into a short story, "Lost Boys," and later a novel of the same name. Although essentially ghost stories, they are also, Card says, "the most autobiographical, personal, and painful" stories he has ever written.[17]

In fact, the short-story version of "Lost Boys," published in *The Magazine of Fantasy and Science Fiction* in October 1989, is written in the first person. In it, Card writes, "I was happy enough about my job—I just wasn't sure I wanted a job at all . . . moving to Greensboro . . . meant I had failed. I had no way of knowing that my career as a fiction writer wasn't over. Maybe I'd be editing and writing books about computers for the rest of my life. Maybe fiction was just a phase I had to go through before I got a *real* job."

He and Kristine loved the city. "Greensboro was a beautiful town, especially to a family from the western desert," he writes in "Lost Boys." "Kristine and I fell in love with it at once."[18]

However, Card did not fall in love with the job at *Compute!* "I was extremely well suited to do the job at *Compute!*," he says. "I was a very good book editor. . . . I produced first-rate work. . . . When I work for somebody, I produce. I just hate working for somebody."[19]

Although he got along with most of the staff at *Compute!*, he did not get along with his two immediate bosses. He also did not like the schedule.

Success at *Compute!* Books, he writes in "Lost Boys," meant giving up a few things—like seeing your children. "I had expected to edit books written by people who couldn't write. What astonished me was that I was editing books about computers written by people who couldn't *program*."[20]

As a result, he spent more time rewriting programs than editing books, working twelve hours or more a day, living on snack food, and hardly seeing his children.

That lifestyle was hard on Kristine, as well. She had two small children to look after and was pregnant with a third, and for the past few years, her husband had mostly been at home. Now he was gone every day.

And then life became even more challenging, with the birth on July 28, 1983, of the Cards' third child, Charles Benjamin. The new baby struggled for life, spending his first few weeks in intensive care, but eventually Charles—Charlie Ben, as he came to be called—came home to be with his parents and older brother and sister.

"Our task was to give him a reason to stay with us," Card wrote. "We stretched and rubbed his limbs, his fingers. We sang to him, talked to him, ignoring the fact that he could not respond to us, assuming instead that the child inside this body was feeling things he could not show.

"And he responded. He awoke. He learned to eat. He recognized our voices. And, many months later than other children, he learned to smile."[21]

Card's job at *Compute!* Books would last just

nine months. Tom Doherty, editor of Tor books, offered Card a contract for his proposed *Alvin Maker* series, and Card quit his job.

Tom Doherty, Card notes, "then had six of my books under contract (*Ender's Game*, *Speaker for the Dead*, three Alvin Maker books, and a story collection) though not one had yet been published. His faith in me—an author whose books, up to then, had never earned out their advances—was extraordinary, and will always be appreciated."[22]

Despite quitting his job at *Compute!*, Card kept his family in Greensboro. "I have a wandering foot. Left to myself, I probably would have moved," Card says. "But Charlie Ben needed the facilities they had for kids with CP [cerebral palsy]."[23]

So for more than two decades now, Greensboro has been the Cards' hometown. And it was in Greensboro that Card would write the book that would elevate his freelance career to a previously undreamed-of level: *Ender's Game*.

## Chapter 7

# Triumph and Tragedy

To briefly recap the details of the genesis of *Ender's Game*, in 1983, Barbara Bova, Card's agent, sold the outline for a novel called *Speaker of Death* to Tom Doherty at the new publishing company Tor Books. As Card began working on the book, he realized it should include a grown-up Andrew "Ender" Wiggin from the "Ender's Game" short story—but that he first needed to expand Ender's story from short story to novel. Tom Doherty agreed, and Card wrote *Ender's Game* very quickly, over December and January of 1983–1984. It was published in 1985—and went on to win the Hugo and Nebula Awards for best novel in 1986, the 1986 Edmund Hamilton-Leigh Brackett Award, and the 1986 Science Fiction Chronicle Readers' Poll Award.[1] And after *Speaker*

*For the Dead* (the new title of *Speaker of Death*) appeared in 1986, it won the 1987 Nebula and Hugo Awards. It was the first time science fiction's top awards had both been won in consecutive years by the same author.

Both books, and the other books set in the "Enderverse" that have followed—*Xenocide* (1991) and *Children of the Mind* (1996) were sequels to *Ender's Game*; *Ender's Shadow* (1999) is set at the same time as *Ender's Game* but focuses on a different character, and has its own sequels, *Shadow of the Hegemon* (2001), *Shadow Puppets* (2002), and *Shadow of the Giant* (2005)—were, and have continued to be, extremely successful.

Card has written extensively about *Ender's Game* over the years, and why he believes the novel has been so popular, but he boils it down to this: "I believe that *Ender's Game* deals with core human dilemmas: the sense of being alone even when surrounded by friends; of being lied to and not knowing whom to believe; of longing to have our actions make some difference in the world, but then being appalled at the responsibility when they do."[2]

*Ender's Game* and *Speaker for the Dead*, remarkable though they were, were not all that Card produced during the late 1980s. Remember, it was actually on the strength of his sale of his proposed "Tales of Alvin Maker" series to Tor Books that he quit his unsatisfactory job at *Compute!* Books to resume full-time freelancing. The first book in the series, *Seventh Son,* was published in 1987. What became the first five chapters of the book, published in *Isaac Asimov's Science Fiction Magazine* in August 1986 as the novella "Hatrack River," was a 1986 Nebula Award finalist, a 1987 Hugo Award finalist, and winner of the 1987 World Fantasy Award.

The stories of the Enderverse are science fiction, set in a distant future of space travel and interstellar war; the Alvin Maker books are fantasy set in agrarian America in the early nineteenth century. (Switching between science fiction and fantasy has never troubled Card. As he puts it, "fantasy has trees, and science fiction has rivets. That's it, that's all the difference there is, the difference of feel, perception.")[3]

Alvin's America is, however, very different from our own. In his version of America, people have "knacks," magical abilities such as dowsing (finding underground water) and the laying on of hands (healing). There are also historical differences between Alvin's America and ours. For example, in Alvin's world, the English Commonwealth still rules, and the king lives in exile in the Crown Colonies, specifically Charleston, South Carolina. (Actually, the English Commonwealth was the brief republican government in England after the English Civil War and the execution of Charles I in 1649. It only lasted until 1653 and was followed by the two protectorates of Oliver Cromwell and his son Richard Cromwell. The English Commonwealth was briefly revived in 1659–1660, and then was abolished with the restoration of the monarchy in the person of Charles II in May 1660.)[4]

"The Alvin stories are set in an alternative America, in which I play games with American history in order to clarify important issues and to allow room for folk magic beliefs to be real," Card says. "The story is about human beings, but along the way it is also about America—its good possibilities and its risks and dangers and evils as well."[5]

Like *Ender's Game*, the Alvin Maker books began with a shorter work—not a short story, but an epic poem, written while Card was in graduate school at the University of Utah, studying the works of the English poet Edmund Spenser. Inspired by Spenser's great masterpiece, *The Faerie Queene*, Card decided to try to do something similar. His poem begins, "Alvin, he was a blacksmith's prentice boy/He pumped the bellows and he ground the knives." Although the poem is incomplete, it won a state fine arts contest in Utah.

"I fell in love with that hill-country voice and the American frontier magic I had devised for the story," Card says. "Here was a fantasy that was completely American—no elves, no dragons, no European myths and legends. . . . I wanted to go back and finish it."[6]

*Seventh Son*, coming right on the heels of *Ender's Game* and *Speaker for the Dead*, cemented Card's reputation. It was a finalist for the 1988 Hugo Award and a finalist for the 1988 World

Fantasy Award, and won the Locus Award for best fantasy novel (voted on by the readers of the science fiction field's primary news and review magazine, *Locus*). It also won him a new legion of fans, who continued to follow Alvin's adventures through the other books in the original trilogy (*Red Prophet*, 1988, and *Prentice Alvin,* 1989) and three additional books since then, *Alvin Journeyman*, (1995) *Heartfire* (1998), and *The Crystal City* (2003).

As Michael Collings notes in *Storyteller: The Official Orson Scott Card Bibliography*, *Seventh Son* was important for another reason. "In this book, for the first time in his science fiction novels, Card not only acknowledges but consciously examines his Mormon heritage," Collings writes. "The story of Alvin Maker provides an analog to the story of Joseph Smith. . . . While non-Mormon readers generally found much of interest and excitement in the novel, Mormon readers consistently discovered much more—they found *their* history, *their* story, *their* epic."[7]

In between *Ender's Game* and *Speaker for the Dead,* Card wrote *Wyrms*, which began life as a novella called "Unwyrm" for an anthology being edited by George R. R. Martin. "I discovered it simply would not stay under 40,000 words," Card says. The novella, as sold, ended up being a shorter version missing several important plot elements, but it never saw print: the publisher, Blue Jay Books, collapsed.[8] The full-length novel version appeared in 1987, at about the same time as *Seventh Son* but from a different publisher (Arbor House instead of Tor Books), which nicely demonstrated Card's ability to write many different tales in many different ways. Reviewer Faren Miller compared the two books in *Locus*: "Where *Seventh Son* is innovative, *Wyrms* is idiosyncratic, a science fiction fable in which Card unleashes an imagination capable of dark grotesqueries far removed from the humane warmth of his Americana."[9]

The next year, 1988, saw the reprint of *A Woman of Destiny* under Card's original title, *Saints*—and Card's first book about writing, *Characters and Viewpoint*, which grew out of a three-part series of articles Card wrote for *Writer's Digest* magazine in 1986.

Card, who is recognized as a master of characterization, attributes his strengths in that area to his early work in the theater. "In the theater, playwrights, directors and actors are all concerned with motivation," he says. "Why does a character do what he does? What is he thinking that motivates him to the actions called for in the script? . . . I approach my characters the same way. I let the reader see what they are thinking. I tell the reader what the character intends to accomplish with his actions. Then if things don't work out as planned, I share the character's distress with my readers."[10]

*Treason*, the extensively revised new edition of *A Planet Called Treason*, also came out in 1988. Then, in 1989, Card published *The Folk of the*

*Fringe*, a collection of stories focusing on the remnants of the Mormon Church, which becomes the primary source of remaining social and cultural stability, after a limited nuclear exchange has devastated the Earth.

Throughout the 1980s, Card continued to write works intended specifically for the Mormon market, including audioplays and animated videoplays for Living Scriptures in Ogden, Utah.

Card has noted that when he began writing science fiction, even though all of his early writing was explicitly Mormon, he made a deliberate choice to exclude religious concerns from his writing. "No one was going to be a member of the Mormon Church; there were going to be no tales of prophets, saviors, priests, or believers. I was going to write pure, unmixed sci-fi."[11]

But oddly, he says, he discovered that his work became more, not less, religious when he stopped dealing with religious subjects consciously. Card realized he was writing religious fiction whether he wanted to or not.

So Card began to give *his* characters a religious life. *Speaker for the Dead* features a colony on another planet in which Brazilian Catholicism is the established church (Card could draw on his experience as a missionary in Brazil in describing that community). But it was in *The Folk of the Fringe* that Card finally "dealt explicitly with Mormon characters and Mormon culture in a near-future setting."[12]

Card rounded out the decade with yet another

first for his career: the book version of *The Abyss*, a blockbuster underwater science-fiction movie directed by James Cameron (who would go on to direct another watery blockbuster, *Titanic*). Cameron and Card wrote in an afterword that they hoped the book would stand as a novel, not just a novelization. Michael Collings, at least, feels it succeeded: "The novel transcends stereotypic action-adventure science fiction . . . through the complex characterization developed by Card's imaginative treatment of Cameron's screenplay," he wrote.[13]

Among the unusual (for film novelizations) steps Card took (with Cameron's permission) was writing three chapters that took place before the beginning of the movie, explaining the background of some of the characters, and inventing details about the movie's aliens, which the film itself leaves mysterious. "I convinced him that what can be mysterious in movies must be explained in written sci-fi," Card says.[14]

Card laughs off the suggestion he undertook the novelization as a way of making money. "Do you have any idea the pathetic amounts of money they pay novelizers? I make ten times the normal on my books." Novelizers also do not get the usual royalties and foreign sales, he points out. "I sacrificed to do that because I believed in Jim Cameron's script and he and I wanted to prove that you could actually adapt film into a good book. We proved it to our satisfaction but we'll never do it again."[15]

Certainly Card will never do it again with James Cameron. Asked about the experience years later, Card replied, "Let's just say that if I wanted to go to hell, there are easier ways than working on a Jim Cameron movie."[16]

By the end of the 1980s, Card had made very clear that he was not going to be pigeonholed: he would, and could, write about anything that interested him, and do so successfully.

That pattern continued through the 1990s. Another book about writing, *How to Write Science Fiction and Fantasy*, came out from *Writer's Digest* Books in 1990—and won Card yet another Hugo Award (for best related book) in 1991. The first edition of *Maps in a Mirror: The Short Fiction of Orson Scott Card*, appeared that same year, containing almost all of Card's short fiction to that time (except for the stories that made up *The Folk of the Fringe*), along with fascinating introductions and afterwords to each group of stories. "Eye for Eye," a novelette which originally appeared in *Isaac Asimov's Science Fiction Magazine* in March 1987 (and won a Hugo Award in 1988) was published as part of a "double novel" alongside Lloyd Biggle Jr.'s "Tunesmith." *The Worthing Saga*, the final, extensively revised version of the stories that originally appeared in *Capitol*, *Hot Sleep,* and *The Worthing Chronicle*, also appeared.

Card also edited the anthology *Future on Fire*, which appeared in 1991 (a companion volume, *Future on Ice*, came out in 1998) and contained, in his view, the best science fiction of the 1980s. He was in a good position to make such a selection: beginning in 1979 he reviewed short fiction for *Science Fiction Review* (his columns ran under the title "You Got No Friends in This World"), and in 1987 he began reviewing books for *The Magazine of Fantasy and Science Fiction* in a column ("Books to Look For") that would continue through the summer of 1993.

Then, in 1992, three books of particular note appeared. The first was *The Memory of Earth*, volume one of a new five-volume science fiction series called "Homecoming." Card sold the series to Tor Books as a "science fictional retelling of the storyline of the Book of Mormon."

"The editor (Beth Meacham) knew what she was buying," Card emphasizes. "I made no effort to preserve the doctrinal preachings, only the human relationships and the conflicts and struggles among the people. But I changed the setting into a separately developed future, so that more than half the story is stuff I made up. In fact, the second volume covers barely a hundred words of the history in the Book of Mormon itself.

"Nobody will be converted to Mormonism by reading the Homecoming series. My hope is that people will be intrigued and entertained by the lives of the people they find there; but that is what I hope for with all my fiction."[17]

The Homecoming series continued with *The Call of Earth,* which also appeared in 1992, *The Ships of Earth* (1994), *Earthfall* (1995), and *Earthborn* (1995).

The other book that came out in 1992 was *Lost Boys*, the novel version of the earlier short story. Unlike the short story, the characters in the novel do not have the same names as the Card family. But many of the family situations were drawn directly from Card's own experiences in the move to Greensboro and Charles Benjamin's cerebral palsy.

"*Lost Boys* is intensely autobiographical," Card says. "So much so that it became too emotional, and I will never do it again. While the climactic events never happened in our family, most of the lesser details did, and the oldest son was based on my oldest son, Geoffrey (who is very much alive and designing electronic games in Seattle). Imagining his death was too painful; it was only bearable because at the time I had not yet lost a child. Now I could never write that book."[18]

*Lost Boys* was the first contemporary novel—that is, a novel set in modern-day America—Orson Scott Card would write, but not the last, as he continued to explore new territory in his writing.

In 1993, *A Storyteller in Zion* was published; it was a collection of Card's written and spoken thoughts about Mormonism and the place of art and fiction within it.

Then, in 1994, came another "first": his first collaboration with another novelist (a very different form of collaboration than his work with James Cameron on the novelization of *The Abyss*). *Lovelock: The Mayflower Trilogy, Book I*, was a joint effort with Kathryn Kidd.

Card's next novel, *Pastwatch: The Redemption of Christopher Columbus*, which came out in 1996, was originally intended to appear in 1992 for the 500th anniversary of Columbus's arrival in the New World. In it, future time travelers, given the chance to alter only a single episode in the past, decide Columbus's discovery of the Americas was the single worst moment in human history and set out to stop it, only to discover it was in fact engineered by other time travelers to preclude something even worse. Their attempted compromise results in an alternative version of American history, another opportunity for Card to imagine how different our world might have turned out. Card envisioned *Pastwatch* as the first book in yet another series

The same year *Pastwatch* appeared, Card's second novel with a contemporary setting, *Treasure Box*, was also published. According to Michael Collings, it represented a conscious effort on Card's part to break into a new genre. Although *Lost Boys* was a ghost story, the "horror" elements were kept to a minimum because of the focus on the characters and community described in the book. In *Treasure Box*, though, "for the first time, Card sets out to write contemporary horror, a ghost story complete with haunted house, eerily deserted graveyard, witches and succubi . . . and he succeeds."[19]

And then, in 1997, came *Stone Tables*, a fictionalized account of the life of Moses, who, as recounted in the Bible, led the Israelites out of slavery in Egypt and (after forty years in the wilderness) to the promised land of Canaan. *Stone Tables* was based on a musical play Card wrote in collaboration with composer Robert Stoddard (a CD of the music was released at about the same time as the novel), first produced at Brigham Young University in 1973.

*Stone Tables* was only the first book Card would write based on Biblical characters. *Sarah*, the first book in the Women of Genesis series, appeared in 2000, followed by *Rebekah* in 2001 and *Rachel & Leah* in 2004.

Card's next two novels (not counting volume five of the Alvin Maker series, *Heartfire*) were both contemporary fantasy. *Homebody* is a ghost story (not really a horror novel, although it was marketed that way), while *Enchantment* is the story of what happens when a modern man finds Sleeping Beauty still asleep in Russia, and wakes her. Both take place primarily in modern-day America. "Strange lands and cultures are wonderful to invent or visit in my fiction, but sometimes I have stories to tell in my own time and place," Card says. "I'm just glad when a publisher is willing to take a chance on a writer who is moving 'out of genre.'"[20] Card has written another contemporary fantasy, *Magic Street*, published in 2005. Set in Los Angeles, it is the story of a foundling child with strange powers.

Card moved even further "out of genre," in a way, with *Magic Mirror*, also published in 1999:

it is a picture book for adults, beautifully illustrated by Nathan Pinnock.

Another "out-of-genre" effort, but one that marked Card's return to his playwriting roots, was the 1997 musical *Barefoot to Zion*.

"I wrote *Barefoot to Zion* with my composer brother, Arlen Card, as our contribution to the LDS Church's celebration of the sesquicentennial of the entry of the pioneers into Salt Lake Valley," Card says,[21] adding that Arlen wrote "Broadway-worthy music that made my lyrics sound better than they are."[22] The musical played to sold-out houses.

The 1990s were, obviously, busy and productive times for Card professionally. Being a professional writer means not just writing, but supporting that writing through promotional activities: speaking tours, autographing sessions, convention appearances, and more. Meanwhile, his children were growing up and he was busy with church activities (as was Kristine: every lay Mormon is supposed to have a "calling," some significant task he or she performs for the church).

But wonderful though those years were in many ways, they were also touched by tragedy.

In the afterword to the short story "Lost Boys," in *Maps in the Mirror*, Card notes that at the Sycamore Hill Writers Workshop in 1988, Karen Fowler told him that by putting the story in first person, he had appropriated something he should not have. "You've pretended to feel the grief of a parent who has lost a child, and you don't have a right to feel that way," he quotes her as saying.

Karen's words, Card says, made him realize what "Lost Boys" was really about: not his fictional eldest child, "Scotty," but his real-life youngest child, Charles Benjamin: Charlie Ben.

"Charlie, who in the five and a half years of his life has never been able to speak a word to us," Card wrote. "Charlie, who could not smile at us until he was a year old, who could not hug us until he was four . . . able to wriggle but not to run, able to call out but not to speak, able to understand that he cannot do what his brother and sister do, but not to ask us why. In short, a child who is not dead and yet can barely taste life despite all our love and all our yearning."

"Lost Boys," Card suggested, was his way of grieving, of removing the mask he had donned, "a mask of calm and acceptance so convincing that I believed it myself." And that, in turn, was why Card found "Lost Boys," both the short story and the novel, "the most personal, painful story of my career."[23]

The entire Card family cared and nurtured Charlie as he grew older. Although some experts told the family Charlie must be mentally challenged because he did not respond the way they expected him to, the Cards knew the experts were wrong—and time proved they were correct, as Charlie developed his own methods of communication.

"Geoffrey was five, about to start school, and

Emily was nearly three when Charlie Ben was born. He grew up in the shelter of their protective care," Card later wrote. "They learned what he needed and watched over him, alerting their parents when they saw him in need, or helping him themselves, when it was within their power."[24]

But Charlie's needs, greater than that of a normal child, put a strain on the family—and especially on Kristine. "I had prided myself on having matched her diaper for diaper, waking for waking, bath for bath when the other children were little," Card wrote. "But we quickly learned that Charlie's needs were so much greater that I could not bear an equal share and still keep up the work that paid the rent."[25]

When Charlie was five, the family got help. Kristine was working in a church program with Erin Absher, who came to her one day and said she felt a strong desire to get to know Charlie. Because she and her new husband, Phillip, did not have any children yet, she felt she had the time to learn how to help with Charlie's needs.

Her help proved vital shortly thereafter, when Kristine suffered a potentially fatal tubal pregnancy that took a long time to recover from. "She could not lift Charlie, and while I could and did take care of him, my work stopped cold while I did so," Card wrote.[26]

Erin Absher began to take care of Charlie almost full-time, living with the Cards during the week. Essentially, Erin became a co-parent, and her help made it possible for the Cards to travel as a family—Charlie included. Despite his handicaps, Charlie traveled overseas, saw plays on Broadway, and visited the beach in Hawaii. In Greensboro, he attended Gateway Education Centre, and had many good experiences there. "The first time he found himself in a room with other children who were also in wheelchairs, he burst out in joyful laughter that he could scarcely contain," Card wrote. "There were others like him! He was not the only one!"[27]

Despite his physical problems, Charlie became a cheerful, bright child who won the hearts of those who met him. "It was Charlie himself who won our hearts, the bright awareness of his eyes, the cheerfulness with which he greeted the world," Card wrote. "Goodness sees goodness as beauty. The people drawn to him recognized his open offer of love and returned it generously."[28]

The Cards' fourth child, Zina Margaret, was born on April 8, 1994. In 1996, Kristine became pregnant again, and as soon as the Cards knew the baby would be a girl, they decided to name her Erin Louisa. "Erin was a family name—for Erin Absher was family now," Card wrote.[29]

But Erin Louisa Card died the day she was born, on March 16, 1997. She is buried in American Fork, Utah. Erin Absher spoke at her funeral. Phillip Absher dedicated the gravesite.

Three years later, on August 16, 2000, the whole Card family—the Abshers included—were at Myrtle Beach, South Carolina. It was the first time that they had all been together in four years:

Card and Kristine, the Abshers, the Cards' oldest son, Geoffrey, home from his mission and college, their oldest daughter, Emily, just on the verge of going off to college, younger daughter Zina—and Charlie.

Charlie enjoyed the sun and being together with his whole family. He did not show any signs of distress. But in the middle of the afternoon, after being taken back to his room, he quietly died.[30]

He was buried beside Erin Louisa in American Fork, Utah, "because we knew that no matter where else family members might move, we would always return, from time to time, to Utah," Card says.[31]

The Cards take comfort in their faith. Although "Faith doesn't stop you from feeling grief," Card says, "grief doesn't stop you from living by faith."[32]

Card's tribute to his son, "The Life of Charlie Ben," posted on his Web site, closes with this strong expression of faith: "It is not merely in our shared memory of his life that Charlie Ben continues, for he lives himself, in the company of his sister Erin Louisa who went before; and he will rise again by the gift of Christ, who surely greeted our dear young man with joy when he came home, and said to him, 'Well done, my good and faithful servant.'"[33]

And today, when the Cards are asked how many children they have, they always say "five."

# Chapter 8

# The Writing Life

Card continues to be as prolific as ever and as wide-ranging in his choice of projects. One of his latest books is the contemporary fantasy *Magic Street*. After that, "I have another contemporary fantasy novel under contract with Del Rey," Card says. "There are two more Women of Genesis novels under contract with Deseret Book, along with a nonfiction book called *Marriage and Civilization*. With Tor, I have a couple more books in the Ender universe, two more *Pastwatch* novels, one more Alvin Maker (*Master Alvin*), two more *Mayflower* books, and a story collection. I'm also writing some comic book series and have written screenplays and plays and probably will again. I contemplate a book on hymns and hymn-writing. Beyond that, I have no particular plans."[1]

Card says he writes in many different fields because "I didn't begin as a novelist and it simply never occurred to me to do only one kind of writing. . . . Writing in just one form would be kind of boring after a while."[2]

He does note, though, that for all the diversified types of writing he does, there's one kind he will probably never be able to sell: "straight mainstream stuff." Publishers, he says, are not interested in his writing unless it contains some supernatural element. "So . . . I tell ghost stories. I tell stories I care about and believe in—but some stories I would love to tell I can not afford to write and publish."

And that is one reason he has delved into the world of screenplays. "In film, you aren't so locked in. . . . There's less of a chance of getting something produced at all—but more of a chance of not getting locked into writing only one kind of thing."[3]

One screenplay he has written is for the movie version of *Ender's Game*, which has been in development for several years. In 2003, Card gave Warner Brothers his version of the script, based on the events in the novels *Ender's Game* and *Ender's Shadow*. As of mid-2005, Wolfgang Petersen, famed director of movies such as *Das Boot* and *Troy*, was slated to direct, and David Benioff, who wrote *Troy*, was working with writing partner D.B. Weiss and Petersen on the newest version of the script.[4]

Card has other film projects in various stages of

development (one of which is a movie version of his book *Homebody*), many of them with Taleswapper, a Los Angeles-based production company of which he is one of the principals (the others are Peter Johnson and Aaron Johnston).[5]

His first venture in writing illustrated novels is the comic series *Ultimate Iron Man* for Marvel. Dabel Pro is also publishing graphic novels based on *Wyrms* and *Red Prophet*.

He continues to offer occasional writing workshops. He recently committed himself to a long-term relationship with Southern Virginia University, where he teaches writing and literature.[6]

Despite his extensive and varied output, Card does not feel he is very disciplined as a writer. Asked what his average day is like, he replies, "I get up. I think about exercising. I put it off. But because I'm going to exercise, I don't work. I read the paper. Play videogames. Watch something on AMC or TCM. Then I exercise. By then most of the day is shot. I play more videogames. I shower. I have dinner. No point in starting writing anything. I go to a movie or hang out with my family or play more videogames or watch more TV. I go to bed and lie awake reading or doing cryptic crosswords until two or three or four. Or five or six. Then I sleep. That's my *average* day. On rare days, I write. When the book is done, I go back to average days."[7]

As a result, he says he does not *feel* prolific. "I'm keenly aware that if I could ever find the discipline to work steadily, I could write six books a year. My total of less than two a year tells you exactly how unsteadily I work."[8]

When he *is* writing, however, he works hard. "I wish I were one of those mature, disciplined writers who produce a certain number of words or pages, or who write for a certain number of hours every day," he says. "Unfortunately, I have to hold the entire thing in my head all at once. I can't walk away from it and do something else until the book is done. In fact, I can barely do anything else. . . . My friends and family enjoy my company a great deal more when I'm not writing."[9]

**"My friends and family enjoy my company a great deal more when I'm not writing."**

**—Orson Scott Card**

Writing a novel, Card says, takes him "three to four weeks of solid typing"—but "three to five years of thought and development."

"I usually have a dozen or more story ideas under serious development in my mind as I read and research and jot down ideas and outline elements," he says.[10]

"I plan major events and research those books where there's something to research. . . . I have to know the ending in order to know where to begin. But I also make up most of the best stuff during the process, as I invent details in passing that grow as I become intrigued with them. I write when I know what to write, and don't write when I don't know yet what I'm doing."

Because of that, he says, "I write final draft, first time. If I find that I have begun improperly, I throw it away and start over from a different place or from a different point of view. I don't fiddle—the best prose is the spontaneous prose, and only when there's an obvious typo or I have inadvertently written unclearly or ambiguously do I edit. I never rewrite."[11]

Which is not to say he never struggles with a story. "Always, though, it's because I was about to make a mistake, and if I just hold off and think about it and wrestle with it and think of new ways to approaching it, I always figure out a way to do it, if not right, then at least adequately."[12]

Once a story is written, he shows it to Kristine. When teaching writing, Card urges writers to find a "wise reader," someone close to them who is also an excellent critic and as committed to their success as they are. He says he turned Kristine into his "wise reader" very early in their marriage.

"Because of her responses and concerns, my work is many times better than it would otherwise have been," he says. "Also, she's part of every page of every story I wrote—instead of my writing being a point of conflict in our marriage, as it is for many other writers, it's one of the places where we're most closely involved with each other."[13]

Card writes (when he is at home in Greensboro) in an attic room. The window looks out on trees and the neighbor's roof. "Occasional wasp's nests and spiderwebs over the years have enlivened the view," he says. "Years' worth of clutter show great promise for excavation by some future archaeologist."[14]

He uses a computer for everything he writes except poetry and song lyrics.[15] He listens to music constantly.

"I can't write in a sound vacuum," he says. His tastes are "eclectic," ranging from Brazilian to jazz (Diana Krall, Jane Monheit), from classic rock like the Eagles to folk-rock like Neil Young, from Bach and other classical composers to Broadway show tunes new and old.

Card says he associates particular pieces of music with every book or story he has written. "I wrote *Enchantment* under the spell of Bruce Cockburn's 'The Charity of Night' and my novel *Lost Boys* was infused with Springsteen's *The Wild, the Innocent, and the E Street Shuffle*—not to mention The Police's 'Every Breath You Take.' During the months after my son died, when I pushed through and finished a novel anyway, the music that sustained me was John Huntington's album of Christmas carols by Robert Stoddard, *December Tales*."[16]

One form of music he does not listen to while writing is rap; he finds it too distracting. "Rap, unfortunately, doesn't function as music for me—it demands attention like shouted poetry, only as poetry it rarely scans well and the topics are usually boring."[17]

Being a writer also means promoting that writing, through speaking tours, autograph sessions, and conferences appearances. Card enjoys meeting his readers, but he does not like spending a lot of time away from his family.

Early in 2001, during his signing tour for *Shadow of the Hegemon*, Card announced that, for several reasons, it would be his last. (He still does individual bookstore signings when he can arrange one in a city he is visiting.) One, he said, was his age (he is now in his 50s), which has affected his resilience and stamina. He had a cold during that tour, and it showed him how quickly he can break down—and how slowly he recovers.

Second, he said he was finding it harder to be away from his family. As the official announcement put it, "The years that parents have with their children are precious, and to spend two solid weeks in which he is not there when his six-year-old comes home from school is even more frustrating now than it has been in the past. Plenty of other people have to make such sacrifices in order to earn a living, but OSC doesn't actually have to, and he won't."[18]

Finally, during signing tours, for weeks just before and for about a week after, he could not write anything substantial.

"I enjoy the actual signings, the chance to meet those who read my books and hear what they care about and look for in the work I do," Card says. "It's the surrounding problems, like jet lag, lost

Orson Scott Card is photographed here with members of the faculty and student body at University Laboratory High School in Illinois during a visit in 1998.

sleep, lack of real exercise, and being away from home, that are taking too high a toll."[19]

Touring required him to be away from his family for as much as a month at a time. "But then," he says, "sometimes I hang around the house and do fun stuff so much that I don't get the work done, and that doesn't have very happy results either." Nevertheless, he says, "By and large, writing as a career has allowed me far more time with my family than I would ever have had with a nine-to-five job."[20]

His youngest daughter, Zina, lives at home, attends school in Greensboro, and likes to play videogames and chess. His son, Geoffrey, is married to Heather Heavener Card, a tutor and substitute teacher, and lives near Seattle. He is an electronic game designer for Amaze Entertainment, publisher of titles such as *Samurai Jack: The Shadow of Aku* and *Shark Tale*. Card's eldest daughter, Emily, is an actress, poet, singer, and audio producer in Los Angeles.[21]

Stopping long book tours has not stopped Card from keeping in touch with his many fans. One of his principal methods of doing so is through an extensive online presence—appropriate for someone who has been involved with the computer world for more than twenty years.

Card's first online presence was on Prodigy; then, unhappy with Prodigy, he switched to AOL and finally moved to the World Wide Web, where he started up three sites.

*Hatrack River* is his author site and the first place to go when you want to know anything about Card. In addition to the latest news, there are interviews, a bibliography, a research section for students, discussion, forums and more. *Nauvoo* is "A Gathering Place for Latter-day Saints." Taleswapper.net is the home for Card's film company, Taleswapper.[22]

Other sites have been added since. *Lost Books* is a site about books that are out of print and forgotten (or, in some cases, back in print—but still forgotten). *Strong Verse* is an online poetry magazine, featuring poetry, new and old, that is meaningful and accessible: its slogan is "Good poetry is meant to be understood, not decoded." *Starshine and Shadows* is the online home of essays on science fiction and fantasy by Michael Collings. Finally, there is *The Ornery American*. "On this website, we look for the voices of those Ornery Americans—the common folk who don't pretend to be intellectuals or elite in any other way, but who are just stubborn enough to think that we ordinary folk are the ones to whom this nation was entrusted from the start," reads the site's description of itself.[23]

"Ornery.org is probably the biggest, but also *Strong Verse* is doing pretty well," Card says. *The Ornery American* features regular essays by Card on various aspects of American life, often (but not always) political. The columns, called "World Watch," appear first in *The Rhinoceros Times*, a weekly newspaper in Greensboro which, says Card, "has a much more conservative viewpoint than I have on many issues, but the editor believes in a free press. (Getting my columns for free, that's what he means by a free press!)."[24]

Also for *The Rhinoceros Times*, Card writes a weekly column called "Uncle Orson Reviews Everything." This is a perfect description because the column includes film reviews, restaurant reviews, book reviews, TV reviews, and more. Once they have been published in *The Rhinoceros Times*, the columns also appear at *Hatrack River*.

The end of long book tours has not meant Card has stopped traveling. As he puts it, Greensboro is only home base: the Cards still travel often. Over the years, their children have accompanied them many times to New York, Los Angeles, Boston, Washington, D.C., and many other U.S. and Canadian cities; they have also visited London,

Paris, Barcelona, Rome, Florence, Berlin, Leipzig, and Jakarta, and spent a summer in France in Provence.

Asked what he does besides writing, Card replies, "For my church, for the past five years, I've been cultural arts director, which largely means putting on plays. I really don't have any hobbies, besides writing my columns of criticism and doing things that give me material to review. I do walk or run most days and enjoy it. And I eat at wonderful restaurants."[25]

## Chapter 9

# The Critical View

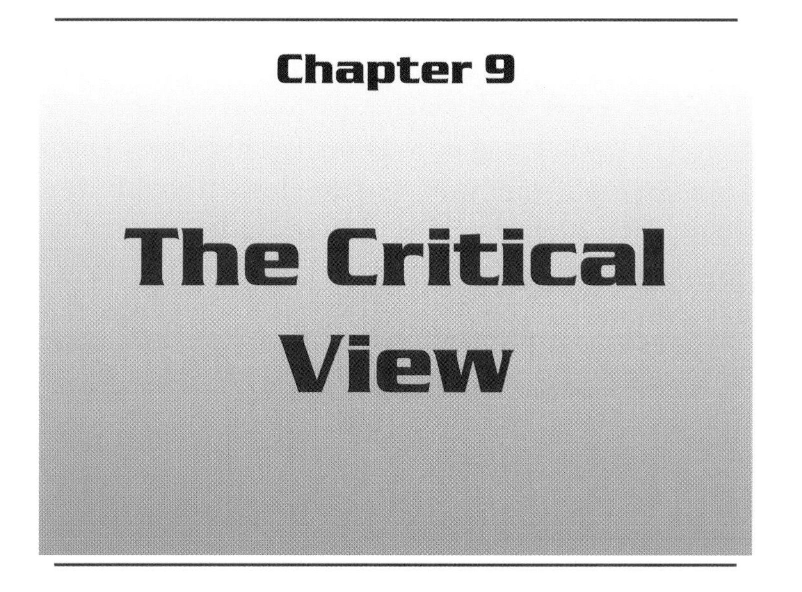

Accusations of "perceived misogyny, gratuitous violence, and graphic cruelty"[1] dogged Card's early work, first surfacing with *A Planet Called Treason*, published in 1979 (and rewritten and re-released as *Treason* in 1988) and continuing in the reaction to his most popular novel, *Ender's Game*.

Card admits there may have been something to the criticisms about his use of violence. "When I read a review where it's clear the person actually understood what was going on in my story, that's very satisfying, but it's also satisfying to read a review where somebody hates my book but they understood what I was doing. That's cool, and I can learn from that," he says. "The complaints about violence in my early work—I hadn't thought I was writing particularly violent work. I realized what I had been doing, without knowing it, was using violence and cruelty as a way of showing that what was going on was really important. Once I understood that was its function, I could stop doing it to such a degree. It's not a tool I rely on anywhere near as frequently as I used to. I wouldn't have known I'd been using it if I hadn't read the review."[2]

Now, he says, "I use the character's own attitude and experiences to let the reader see how important the events are in the character's life. Instead of having the character smacked in the head with a brick, I have the character smacked with an emotional surprise that only *feels* like a brick. Works better, less blood."[3]

Some negative reaction to Card's work seems to be based on disagreements with Card's perceived personal beliefs, both religious and political.

Card says, "One of the great deceptions of contemporary media is that nobody talks or thinks about God when in the real world most people do."[4] He gets both attacked and praised for giving many of his characters a religious life. "Some critics think it's a breath of fresh air to see characters who have a religious and spiritual life and aren't despised by the author because of it. Others, of course, are sure that I'm trying to sneak my insidious Mormon agenda into the minds of poor, stupid readers."[5]

Card says such hostility comes both "from right-wing Christians who think Mormons are the anti-Christ, and from left-wing p.c. [politically correct] 'intellectuals' who think that hating religious people proves how open-minded they are."[6]

People who view his science fiction and fantasy books as "religious fiction" generally take that attitude out of hostility, Card says, "in order to dismiss my books by putting them in a category that they don't have to take seriously."

He adds, "Since my characters also have family relationships to a far greater degree than the rest of American fiction . . . one could just as easily—and far more plausibly—say that I write 'family fiction.'"[7]

Card also gets attacked (and praised) within the Mormon faith. "There are Mormons who love my work and absolutely get what I'm doing. There are Mormons who think I'm the devil. Oddly enough, the latter category is equally divided between leftwing Mormons who think I'm the devil because I'm so rigidly orthodox, and rightwing Mormons who think I'm the devil because I'm so obviously heretical. As long as the hatred is evenly balanced on both sides, I'm probably okay."[8]

He adds, "Because I'm a believing Mormon, there's going to be a lot of Mormon influence in my work; because I'm different from all other Mormons (just as I'm different from all other non-Mormons), there's going to be a lot of stuff in there that other Mormons aren't comfortable or familiar with."[9]

Card's *Ender* books have also been criticized by feminists for not having enough women in them.

## Is Orson Scott Card a science fiction writer?

Card is often identified as a science fiction writer. However, unlike most of the "big-name" science fiction and fantasy writers, he is seldom seen at science fiction conventions, and he is not a member of the Science Fiction and Fantasy Writers of America (SFWA). "I used to be part of the science fiction community, but I was excommunicated long ago," Card says.[10]

The reason for his "excommunication" goes back to the publication of *Ender's Game,* which generated a storm of controversy within the SFWA. "The real *Ender's Game* controversy was the resentment of many people that I got the Nebula Award while I was serving SFWA as the Nebula Awards Report editor," Card says. "Though no NAR editor had ever been nominated while serving, and nobody could even hint at a way my position could have influenced anybody, some ugly things were said by people who should have known better. . . . I didn't make any big announcement . . . All I did was not renew my SFWA membership."[11]

However, he adds, "When I say I left the community, that doesn't change the fact that I have many dear friends there, and many writers I really admire. If America were governed by people with the diversity of the science fiction community, we'd be much better off as a country."[12]

Card counters that such critics "ignore my books that are absolutely built around women: Women of Genesis, *Saints* . . . and books where women play equally important roles, like most of the *Alvin* books and *Lost Boys*. In other words, they look for opportunities to hate my work, [so] it's hardly surprising when they find them." Card feels that is a depressingly common critical approach to his writing. "Most attacks on my work take the strategy of deliberately ignoring most of what I've written so that I can be attacked for not having addressed their particular agenda in a handful of works. I'm scornful of and irritated at such critics, but in the long run, readers will choose between me and them."[13]

Card believes that attacks on his work based on the beliefs expressed in them are off-base because he actually avoids using his fiction to preach his own beliefs. "That would be a waste of time. What is consciously inserted into a story is always noticeable to any but the most naïve reader, and will probably be consciously rejected. Instead, I trust my unconscious choices to reveal what I truly believe—things that I only discover myself when I reread the book or story many years later."[14]

However, the writer who trusts his unconscious mind to express his deepest beliefs, Card notes wryly, runs the risk of having his books influence people "toward what he really believes rather than toward what he believes he believes—and trust me, there is usually a wide gap between those two things in most people."[15]

Card also emphasizes that his characters often have opinions that he disagrees with. "I think it's essential, as a writer, that I tell their stories with absolute honesty and as much depth as I can muster. That would be impossible if I made my characters serve a political agenda."[16]

---

**"[Certain critics] look for opportunities to hate my work, [so] it's hardly surprising when they find them."**

**—Orson Scott Card**

---

Whenever he wants to send a message, either a religious or political one, to deliberately, openly, argue for a position, Card says "I write an essay. I have found I do best just posting them online. . . . What I find interesting is the people who post on my website tend to be people who really disagree with me. At least people who hate what I say are paying attention! It just makes me feel better for having had my say."[17]

Card says his fundamental principles have not really changed over the years. "But as I've learned more about what makes civilization work, I have made firm decisions about topics that I only waffled on at first."[18]

But, he adds, "many of my important beliefs have not been written at all, and won't be until I'm ready. No point in expressing something badly."

"At the same time, I have no guarantee that I'm right about anything," he says. "Whenever you're writing essays about current world events, it's always good to keep the tiniest modicum of humility about the possibility that you may be flat wrong."[19]

Card's books in general—and the "Ender" books in particular—have been taken to heart by young readers everywhere. They have also been taken to heart by teachers. *Ender's Game* is taught in some schools, somewhat to Card's bemusement. "I'm always a bit worried when students are forced to read a book of mine in order to get a grade," he says. "The danger is that the readers will be hostile to the book because of that, and no story can survive a hostile reading. But so far it seems to be doing little harm, and from what I hear, most students actually end up enjoying it."[20]

Tor Books recently re-released *Ender's Game* and *Ender's Shadow* in new editions aimed at the young adult market, but despite their appeal to a younger audience, Card says he has never written "for kids."

"That seems to involve limiting your audience," he says. "I'm always reaching for every possible reader. I have, however, occasionally made small changes in decorum—in *all* my books—to make them more likely to be carried by school libraries. That, too, is part of my desire not to limit my audience because of trivialities like language choice.

"I'm glad when kids read my fiction, because

they're the best and toughest audience. They're not trying to impress anybody, and they give themselves over wholly to stories that they love."

As with most authors, the ultimate critical verdict on the work of Orson Scott Card probably will not be reached until he is long dead. But Card is not really worried about critical verdicts—or even how well his books sell today.

"My audience could disappear tomorrow," he says. "But my children will still be my children. My wife will still be my wife. My friends are still my friends, regardless of what my books do.

"I just think it's better to fail as a writer and succeed as a human being than to succeed as a writer and fail as a human being."[24]

# In His Own Words

The following interview was conducted with Orson Scott Card by the author via e-mail between March 4, 2004 and February 16, 2005.

*What did you read when you were growing up?*

At seven I read *The Prince and the Pauper* (after *Tom Sawyer*, *Little Women, Little Men*, and *Jo's Boys*), which fascinated me with England and English history. I read *Rise and Fall of the Third Reich* when I was ten—devastating, but shaped my moral worldview. My parents gave me *The Army of the Potomac*, the three-volume series by Bruce Catton, when I was ten or eleven, and I learned about real war, not just the cursory stuff we got in school. That was when I learned to love history. I read biographies of doctors and scientists and enough history that I had a very clear idea of the shape of the past, the major civilizations, etc.—and heaven knows I got precious little help in that from school.

Later, it was my older brother who encouraged me to read science fiction—*Catseye* by Andre Norton was a book he lent to me early on; and I found other sci-fi in libraries. But it was never the majority of my reading. Historical novels, mysteries, Jane Austen—ah, Jane Austen!—Charles Dickens: these were the books I read most, and for love.

*You were exposed to music and books from an early age. How much influence did that have on your eventual writing career and interest in the theater?*

I'm not sure. I had the verbal gifts, the concentration, the musical talent that made it so I could do something about books and writing and music and performance when the time came. Would I have discovered them anyway? Probably. But these were the things that connected us to each other and the world around us.

My parents were very news-aware. They were well-read and well-educated (despite my mom's lack of a degree, she's one of the smartest women I've known). They talked about real stuff with us kids, and listened to us as if our opinions mattered. We discussed the books we had read; we discussed movies and TV shows and why some were bad and some were good. We were always highly verbal about everything, and took all the arts very, very seriously. And above all, my parents both seemed to believe that whatever their children wanted to do, they could and *should* do brilliantly. So we were always expected to work our butts off to prepare—and they would work alongside us, devoting time to helping us memorize, make costumes for us, whatever it took. They were both truly and fully devoted to their kids. They believed in us. Yet never pushed us—they first let us decide what we were interested in, then supported those interests and talents any way they could, while insisting on excellence, as much as was within our reach.

### *What prompted you to write your first story (about a smart kid beaten up by bullies)?*

What prompted me was those old fears and my mother's story about the kid who was beaten to the point of brain damage when *she* was in school, along with the family subscription to *Writer's Digest*.

### *Have you ever regretted becoming a freelance writer?*

No, we have no regrets about going freelance. Because I was a freelancer, I was there for the key milestones of my children's lives. They had their dad in the house along with their mom. It was great for us all.

### *How has being a father affected you?*

Before I was a father, I didn't have any children. Afterward, I did. Whether it changed me in any deep way is not for me to judge. Maybe I was always ready to have kids; maybe I'm a lousy father. I'm hardly the one to answer. As to how it affected my writing . . . anyone who has read it knows that fatherhood and parenthood are an important aspect of what I write. I tell stories about people in families or in tightly knit communities. Not loners, like most fiction writers. Is that because I've had children? Maybe. But I grew up in a family, too. Still, the fiction I wrote before I had children was more about people cut off from (important) families, and after that, I wrote more and more about people in families. So . . . coincidence? Natural development of my fiction? Or my life impinging on my art? I don't think about those things when I'm writing, and after I've written something, it's for other people to decide whether they think my life has shaped my art (or vice versa). It's not a question I find interesting about other writers, so I would hardly have dwelt on it myself.

### Why do you think *Ender's Game* has been so popular?

I believe that *Ender's Game* deals with core human dilemmas: the sense of being alone even when surrounded by friends; of being lied to and not knowing whom to believe; of longing to have our actions make some difference in the world, but then being appalled at the responsibility when they do.

### How has its enormous success affected you?

Enormous? That's relative, isn't it? *Harry Potter*: that's enormous success. *Ender's Game* has been generously received by some groups, but Stephen King's slightest work regularly outsells my best. I'm just glad that enough people buy my books that I can keep my household running and have enough extra to do some things that matter to me.

### *Is there pressure to live up to the various awards you've won?*

There's no pressure to "live up to" awards. There's only pressure to come up with really good stories that I and, hopefully, my readers will enjoy, and then write a manuscript that deals with all the problems and tells the story effectively. The thrill of winning an award lasts about ten minutes. Then it's back to work.

### *What do you do when you're not writing?*

For my church, for the past five years, I've been cultural arts director, which largely means putting on plays. I really don't have any hobbies, besides writing my columns of criticism and doing the things that give me material to review. I do walk or run most days and enjoy it. And I eat at wonderful restaurants.

# Chronology

**1951**—Orson Scott Card is born on August 24 in Richland, Washington, to Willard Richards Card and Peggy Jane Park Card.

**1951**—Family moves to San Mateo, California.

**1954**—Family moves to Salt Lake City, Utah.

**1957**—Family moves to Santa Clara, California.

**1961**—Scott writes first story (about a smart kid attacked by bullies); Peggy Card submits it to two magazines; both reject it.

**1964**—Family moves to Mesa, Arizona.

**1967**—Family moves to Orem, Utah. Scott comes up with idea of the Battle Room.

**1968**—Scott graduates from high school (one year early); enters Brigham Young University.

**1969–1971**—Studies theater at BYU. Begins writing plays. Submits "The Tinker" for publication; it is rejected, with encouragement.

**1971**—Meets Kristine Allen.

**1971–1973**—Serves as a Mormon missionary in Sao Paulo, Brazil; writes the musical *Stone Tables*.

**1973**—Returns to BYU.

**1974**—Establishes the Utah Valley Repertory Theatre Company. Writes "Ender's Game." Begins work at BYU Press.

**1975**—Receives bachelor's degree in theater (with distinction). Becomes full-time assistant editor at *The Ensign*, the official magazine of the Church of Jesus Christ of Latter-day Saints. Moves from Provo to Salt Lake City. Utah Valley Repertory Theatre folds.

**1977**—"Ender's Game" (the short-story version) is published in *Analog*. First book, *"Listen Mom and Dad..."*, is published. On May17, marries Kristine Allen.

**1978**—Quits *The Ensign* to become full-time freelance writer. Son Michael Geoffrey is born on April 25. Receives John W. Campbell Award for Best New Science Fiction Writer in September.

**1979**—First three fiction books are published.

**1980**—*Songmaster* is published. Daughter Emily Janice is born on August 17.

**1981**—Receives master's degree from University of Utah. Moves to South Bend, Indiana, to pursue a Ph.D. at the University of Notre Dame.

**1983**—Abandons Ph.D. work. Moves to Greensboro, North Carolina, to work as an editor for *Compute!* Books. Son Charles Benjamin is born on July 28.

**1984**—Quits job at *Compute*! Books. *A Woman of Destiny* is published.

**1985**—Wins Association for Mormon Letters Award for *A Woman of Destiny*. *Ender's Game* (the novel) is published.

**1986**—*Ender's Game* wins the Nebula and Hugo Awards for best novel, plus the Edmund Hamilton/Leigh Brackett Award for best novel. *Speaker for the Dead* (sequel to *Ender's Game*) is published.

**1987**—*Speaker for the Dead* wins Nebula and Hugo Awards for best novel, plus the Locus Award for best novel. Short story "Hatrack River" (first Alvin Maker story) wins World Fantasy Award.

**1988**—Production of *America's Witness for Christ* (The Hill Cummorah Pageant) debuts. *Eye for Eye* wins Hugo Award for best novella and the Japanese Science Fiction Award.

**1989**—*Red Prophet* wins Locus Award for Best Fantasy Novel.

**1991**—*Maps in a Mirror* wins Locus Award for Best Collection.

**1994**—Daughter Zina Margaret is born on April 8.

**1997**—Production of *Barefoot to Zion*, musical written with brother Arlen Card, debuts. *Stone Tables,* novelization of musical play written in Brazil, is published. Daughter Erin Louisa is born, on March 16, but lives just a few hours.

**2000**—Son Charles dies on August 16, while on a family vacation in Myrtle Beach, South Carolina.

# Chapter Notes

## Chapter 1. The Beginnings of *Ender*

1. "OSC Answers Questions, May 12, 2000," *Hatrack River—The Official Website of Orson Scott Card*, <http://www.hatrack.com/research/questions/q0044.shtm> (July 6, 2004).
2. "Other View: Orson Scott Card," n.d., <http://www.jointhesaga.com/otherviews/card.htm> (July 7, 2004).
3. Ibid.
4. Jeff Duke, "Orson Scott Card Interview by Jeff Duke," n.d. <http://www.hatrack.com/research/interviews/1997-jeffduke.shtml> (June 30, 2004).
5. Edith S. Tyson, *Orson Scott Card: Writer of the Terrible Choice*, (Lanham, Md., The Scarecrow Press, Inc., 2003), p. xvii.
6. Grace Anne DeCandido and Keith R.A. DeCandido, "PW Interviews Orson Scott Card," *Publishers Weekly*, November 30, 1990.
7. Duke.
8. "OSC Answers Questions, May 12, 2000."
9. DeCandido.

## Chapter 2. Early Life

1. Edith S. Tyson, *Orson Scott Card: Writer of the Terrible Choice* (Lanham, Md., The Scarecrow Press, Inc., 2003), p. xv.
2. E-mail from Orson Scott Card, March 4, 2004.
3. E-mail from Orson Scott Card, February 4, 2004.
4. E-mail, March 4, 2004.
5. Ibid.

6. *The Church of Jesus Christ of Latter-day Saints Website*, n.d., <http://www.lds.org/newsroom/glossary/0,15400,3904-1-T,00.html> (July 13, 2004).
7. E-mail, March 4, 2004.
8. "Pioneers," *Mormon.org*, n.d., <http://www.mormon.org/learn/0,8672,964-1,00.html>, and "Settling of Salt Lake," *Mormon.org*, n.d., <http://www.mormon.org/learn/0,8672,965-1,00.html> (July 14, 2004).
9. Orson Scott Card E-mail, July 21, 2004.
10. E-mail, March 4, 2004.
11. "Beliefs and Doctrines," *The Church of Jesus Christ of Latter-day Saints Website*, <http://www.lds.org/newsroom/page/0,15606,4030-1—-4-168,00.html> (July 14, 2004).
12. E-mail, March 4, 2004.
13. Ibid.
14. Ibid.


## Chapter 3. School Days


1. Edith S. Tyson, *Orson Scott Card: Writer of the Terrible Choice* (Lanham, Md., The Scarecrow Press, Inc., 2003), p. xv.
2. E-mail from Orson Scott Card, February 4, 2004.
3. Ibid.
4. E-mail from Orson Scott Card, March 4, 2004.
5. "Orson Scott Card Interview," *Hatrack River—The Official Website of Orson Scott Card*, n.d., <http://www.hatrack.com/research/interviews/interview2.shtml> (June 30, 2004).
6. E-mail from Orson Scott Card, April 5, 2004.
7. E-mail from Orson Scott Card, March 4, 2004.

8. "OSC Answers Questions," *Hatrack River—The Official Website of Orson Scott Card*, n.d., <http://www.hatrack.com/research/questions/q0034.shtml> (July 6, 2004).
9. Steven Argyle, "Orson Scott Card—A Literary Maverick," *Main Street Journal*, December 1988, <http://www.hatrack.com/research/articles/1988-steven-argyle.shtml> (February 24, 2004).
10. E-mail from Orson Scott Card, March 4, 2004.
11. "Orson Scott Card—A Literary Maverick."
12. "OSC Answers Questions."
13. "Orson Scott Card—A Literary Maverick."
14. E-mail from Orson Scott Card, March 4, 2004.
15. E-mail from Orson Scott Card, April 5, 2004.
16. E-mail from Orson Scott Card, March 4, 2004.
17. Ibid.
18. Ibid.
19. Ibid.
20. Ibid.
21. E-mail from Orson Scott Card, April 5, 2004.
22. "Orson Scott Card—A Literary Maverick."
23. E-mail from Orson Scott Card, April 5, 2004.
24. E-mail from Orson Scott Card, February 4, 2004.

## Chapter 4. BYU to Brazil and Back

1. E-mail from Orson Scott Card, July 30, 2004.
2. E-mail from Orson Scott Card, April 5, 2004.
3. Ibid.
4. Ibid.
5. Ibid.
6. Ibid.
7. Ibid.
8. Ibid.

9. Ibid.
10. Ibid.
11. "Orson Scott Card Interview," *Hatrack River—The Official Website of Orson Scott Card*, n.d., <http://www.hatrack.com/research/interviews/interview2.shtml> (June 30, 2004).
12. E-mail from Orson Scott Card, April 5, 2004.
13. Ibid.
14. Orson Scott Card e-mail, May 31, 2004.
15. Ibid.
16. Ibid.
17. Ibid.
18. Ibid.
19. Edith S. Tyson, *Orson Scott Card: Writer of the Terrible Choice* (Lanham, Md., The Scarecrow Press, Inc., 2003), p. xvi.
20. Orson Scott Card e-mail, May 31, 2004.
21. Ibid.
22. Ibid.
23. "Kon-Tiki Web: Museum," n.d., <http://www.museumsnett.no/kon-tiki/Expeditions/> (August 3, 2004).
24. Orson Scott Card e-mail, May 31, 2004.
25. Ibid.
26. Ibid.
27. Ibid.
28. Ibid.
29. Ibid.
30. Ibid.
31. Orson Scott Card e-mail, March 4, 2004.
32. Orson Scott Card e-mail, May 31, 2004.
33. Tyson, p. xvii.
34. Orson Scott Card e-mail, May 31, 2004.

## Chapter 5. First Sale and Marriage

1. Orson Scott Card e-mail, May 31, 2004.
2. Orson Scott Card e-mail, June 4, 2004.
3. Ibid.
4. Ibid.
5. GraceAnne A. and Keith R. A. DeCandido, "PW Interviews Orson Scott Card," *Publishers Weekly*, November 30, 1990.
6. Ibid.
7. Ibid.
8. Michael A. Collings, *Storyteller: The Official Orson Scott Card Bibliography and Guide* (Woodstock, Ga.: Overlook Connection Press, 2001), p. 287.
9. Orson Scott Card e-mail, June 4, 2004.
10. Ibid.
11. Ibid.
12. Ibid.
13. Orson Scott Card e-mail, February 25, 2005.
14. Orson Scott Card e-mail, February 4, 2004.
15. Orson Scott Card e-mail, June 4, 2004.
16. Ibid.
17. Collings, pp. 290–293.
18. Mark R. Kelly, *The Locus Index to Science Fiction Awards*, n.d., <http://www.locusmag.com/SFAwards/index.html> (June 21, 2005).
19. Orson Scott Card e-mail, June 4, 2004.
20. Ibid.
21. Bradley Sinor, *Science Fiction & Fantasy Book Review*, April, 1979, p. 27.
22. *Publisher's Weekly*, December 4, 1978, p. 4.
23. Fred Niederman, *Science Fiction and Fantasy Book Review*, December, 1979, p. 155.

24. Michael Bishop, *Magazine of Fantasy & Science Fiction*, January, 1980, p. 35.
25. Collings, p. 47.
26. Scott Nicholson, "Card's Game: An Interview with Orson Scott Card," *Hatrack River—The Official Website of Orson Scott Card*, n.d., <http://www.hatrack.com/research/interviews/1998-scott-nicholson.shtml> (June 30, 2004).
27. Orson Scott Card e-mail, June 4, 2004.
28. Orson Scott Card e-mail, February 16, 2005.
29. Orson Scott Card e-mail, June 4 2004.

## Chapter 6. Children and Challenges

1. "Otherview: Orson Scott Card," *Saga E-zine*, n.d., <http://saga.jointhesaga.com/mt/archives/cat_otherviews.html> (June 10, 2005).
2. Orson Scott Card e-mail, February 16, 2005.
3. "Who is Orson Scott Card?" *Hatrack River—The Official Website of Orson Scott Card*, n.d., <http://www.hatrack.com/osc/about-more.shtml> (June 10, 2005).
4. Orson Scott Card, *Maps in a Mirror: The Short Fiction of Orson Scott Card* (New York: Orb, 2004), pp. 663–664.
5. Ibid., p. 664.
6. Ibid., p. 665.
7. Ibid., p. 666.
8. Michael A. Collings, *Storyteller: The Official Orson Scott Card Bibliography and Guide* (Woodstock, Ga.: Overlook Connection Press, 2001), p. 55.
9. "Who is Orson Scott Card?"
10. Ibid.
11. Orson Scott Card e-mail, February 16, 2005.
12. Ibid.

13. Edith S. Tyson, *Orson Scott Card: Writer of the Terrible Choice* (Lanham, Md., The Scarecrow Press, Inc., 2003), p. xx.
14. Ibid.
15. Ibid.
16. Ibid.
17. Card, *Maps in a Mirror: The Short Fiction of Orson Scott Card*, pp. 130–131.
18. Ibid., "Lost Boys," p. 108.
19. Orson Scott Card e-mail, February 4, 2004.
20. Card, *Maps in a Mirror*, "Lost Boys," p. 109.
21. Orson Scott Card, "The Life of Charles Benjamin Card," *Hatrack River—The Official Website of Orson Scott Card*, n.d., <http://www.hatrack.com/misc/Charlie/bio.shtml> (June 9, 2005).
22. Card, *Maps in a Mirror*, p. 671.
23. Orson Scott Card e-mail, February 16, 2005.

## Chapter 7. Triumph and Tragedy

1. Michael A. Collings, *Storyteller: The Official Orson Scott Card Bibliography and Guide* (Woodstock, Ga.: Overlook Connection Press, 2001), p. 90.
2. Orson Scott Card e-mail, February 16, 2005.
3. Howard Mittelmark, "Orson Scott Card Interview," *Inside Books*, January, 1989, <http://www.hatrack.com/research/articles/1989-01-howard-mittelmark.shtml> (February 24, 2004).
4. "English Commonwealth and Protectorate," *MSN Encarta* (UK), n.d., <http://uk.encarta.msn.com/encyclopedia_781532227/English_Commonwealth_and_Protectorate.html> (November 6, 2005).

5. "OSC interview with a French Magazine, August 2003," *Hatrack River—The Official Website of Orson Scott Card*, <http://www.hatrack.com/research/interviews/2003-french-interview.shtml> (June 30, 2004).
6. Orson Scott Card, *Maps in a Mirror: The Short Fiction of Orson Scott Card* (New York: Orb, 2004), pp. 670–671.
7. Collings, p. 123.
8. Card, *Maps in a Mirror,* pp. 666–667.
9. Faren Miller, "Locus Looks at Books," *Locus*, May 1987, p. 13.
10. Steven Argyle, "Orson Scott Card—A Literary Maverick," *Main Street Journal*, December 1988, <http://www.hatrack.com/research/articles/1988-steven-argyle.shtml> (February 24, 2004).
11. *Maps in a Mirror*, pp. 435.
12. Ibid, pp. 435-438.
13. Collings, p. 168.
14. "OSC interview with a French Magazine, August 2003."
15. Orson Scott Card, "Towards a Mormon Aesthetic," *Mormon Arts Festival 1995 Keynote Address*, <http://www.ldsfilm.com/ar/ar_aesthetic.html> (June 17, 2005).
16. "Readers welcome popular SF writer," Online chat transcript, *CNN.com Interviews*, August 23, 1999, <http://www.cnn.com/books/dialogue/9908/orson.card/> (February 24, 2004).
17. "OSC interview with a French Magazine, August 2003."

18. Ryan Timothy Grable and Christopher Hennessey-DeRose, "There's no end to the writing game for the prolific Orson Scott Card," *Science Fiction Weekly* Interview, n.d., <http://www.scifi.com/sfw/issue328/interview.html> (February 24, 2004).
19. Collings, p. 265.
20. "There's no end to the writing game for the prolific Orson Scott Card."
21. "Orson Scott Card Interview," *Hatrack River—The Official Website of Orson Scott Card*, n.d., <http://www.hatrack.com/research/interviews/interview.shtml> (June 30, 2004).
22. Claire E. White, "A Conversation with Orson Scott Card," *Writers Write—The Internet Writing Journal*, September 1999, <http://www.writerswrite.com/journal/sep99/card.htm> (June 17, 2005).
23. *Maps in a Mirror,* p. 119.
24. Orson Scott Card, "The Life of Charles Benjamin Card," *Hatrack River—The Official Website of Orson Scott Card*, n.d., <http://www.hatrack.com/misc/Charlie/bio.shtml> (June 9, 2005).
25. Ibid.
26. Ibid.
27. Ibid.
28. Ibid.
29. Ibid.
30. Ibid.
31. Orson Scott Card e-mail, February 16, 2005.
32. Orson Scott Card e-mail, February 16, 2005.
33. "The Life of Charles Benjamin Card."

## Chapter 8. The Writing Life

1. Orson Scott Card e-mail, February 24, 2004.

2. "Interview with Orson Scott Card," *America Online*, January 19, 1994, <http://www.hatrack.com/research/interviews/1994-01-aol.shtml> (June 30, 2004).
3. N. L. Thompson, "Orson Scott Card Mailing List Members Get Answers!" *Transcript of Q&A session in Barnes and Noble Forum*, March 20, 1998, <http://www.timp.net/osclistgallery/BNN980320.htm> (February 24, 2004).
4. "News about Ender's Game: The Movie," March 30, 2005, <http://www.frescopictures.com/movies/ender/endersgame_update.htm> (June 20, 2005).
5. Manuscript note to author from Orson Scott Card's assistant, Kathleen Bellamy, received November 3, 2005.
6. "Who is Orson Scott Card?" *Hatrack River—The Official Website of Orson Scott Card*, n.d., <http://www.hatrack.com/osc/about-more.shtml> (June 10, 2005).
7. "Interview with Sonja," *Hatrack River—The Official Website of Orson Scott Card*, n.d., <http://www.hatrack.com/research/interviews/2004-sonja.shtml> (June 9, 2005).
8. Claire E. White, "A Conversation with Orson Scott Card," *Writers Write—The Internet Writing Journal*, September 1999, <http://www.writerswrite.com/journal/sep99/card.htm> (June 17, 2005).
9. GraceAnne A. and Keith R. A. DeCandido, "PW Interviews Orson Scott Card," *Publishers Weekly*, November 30, 1990.
10. "Interview with Orson Scott Card."
11. Orson Scott Card e-mail, February 16, 2005.
12. Ibid.

13. Orson Scott Card, *How to Write Science Fiction & Fantasy* (Cincinnati, Ohio: Writer's Digest Books, 1990), p. 123.
14. "Behind the Words."
15. Orson Scott Card e-mail, February 24, 2005.
16. James Schellenberg, "Under the Influence?" *Strange Horizons*, April 18, 2005, <http://www.strangehorizons.com/2005/20050418/schellenberg-c.shtml> (April 21, 2005).
17. Ryan Timothy Grable and Christopher Hennessey-DeRose, "There's no end to the writing game for the prolific Orson Scott Card," *Science Fiction Weekly* Interview, n.d., <http://www.scifi.com/sfw/issue328/interview.html> (February 24, 2004).
18. "OSC Announces Last Signing Tour," *Hatrack River—The Official Website of Orson Scott Card*, January 6, 2001, <http://www.hatrack.com/news-reviews/news/2002-01-06.shtml> (June 16, 2005).
19. Ibid.
20. Claire E. White, "A Conversation with Orson Scott Card," *Writers Write—The Internet Writing Journal,* September 1999, <http://www.writerswrite.com/journal/sep99/card.htm> (June 17, 2005).
21. "Who is Orson Scott Card?"
22. Orson Scott Card e-mail, February 16, 2005.
23. "Who is the Ornery American?" n.d., <http://www.ornery.org/about.html> (June 20, 2005).
24. "Orson Scott Card: Casting Shadows," *Locus Magazine*, December 2002, p. 71.
25. Orson Scott Card e-mail, February 16, 2005.

## Chapter 9. The Critical View

1. Michael A. Collings, *Storyteller: The Official Orson Scott Card Bibliography and Guide* (Woodstock, Ga.: Overlook Connection Press, 2001), p. 12.
2. "Orson Scott Card: Casting Shadows," *Locus Magazine*, December 2002, p. 72.
3. Tina Morgan, "Interview with Orson Scott Card," *Fiction Factor: The Online Magazine for Fiction Writers,* n.d., <http://www.fictionfactor.com/interviews/OrsonScottCard.html> (February 24, 2004).
4. "Publishers Weekly Talks with Orson Scott Card," *Hatrack River—The Official Website of Orson Scott Card*, November 20, 2000, <http://www.hatrack.com/research/interviews/2000-11-pw.shtml> (June 30, 2004).
5. "Interview with Orson Scott Card," *America Online*, January 19, 1994, <http://www.hatrack.com/research/interviews/1994-01-aol.shtml> (June 30, 2004).
6. Orson Scott Card e-mail, February 16, 2005.
7. "Orson Scott Card Interview," *Hatrack River—The Official Website of Orson Scott Card*, n.d., <http://www.hatrack.com/research/interviews/interview.shtml> (June 30, 2004).
8. Claire E. White, "A Conversation with Orson Scott Card," *Writers Write—The Internet Writing Journal,* September 1999, <http://www.writerswrite.com/journal/sep99/card.htm> (June 17, 2005).
9. "Interview with Orson Scott Card," *America Online*, January 19, 1994.
10. "Orson Scott Card: Casting Shadows,'" p. 71.
11. Orson Scott Card e-mail, February 4, 2004.

12. "Orson Scott Card: Casting Shadows."
13. Orson Scott Card e-mail, February 16, 2005.
14. "OSC interview with a French magazine," *Hatrack River—The Official Website of Orson Scott Card*, August 2003, <http://www.hatrack.com/research/interviews/2003-french-interview.shtml> (June 30, 2004).
15. Ryan Timothy Grable and Christopher Hennessey-DeRose, "There's no end to the writing game for the prolific Orson Scott Card," *Science Fiction Weekly* Interview, n.d., <http://www.scifi.com/sfw/issue328/interview.html> (February 24, 2004).
16. John C. Snider, "Interview: Orson Scott Card," *SciFi Dimensions*, April 2005, <http://www.scifidimensions.com/Apr05/orsonscottcard.htm> (June 9, 2005).
17. "Orson Scott Card: Casting Shadows,"
18. Orson Scott Card e-mail, February 16, 2005.
19. "Orson Scott Card: Casting Shadows," p. 71.
20. Morgan, "Interview with Orson Scott Card."
21. Scott Nicholson, "Orson Scott Card: 'Learn Everything About Everything,'" *Ghostwriter,* n.d., <http://www.hauntedcomputer.com/ghostwr22.htm> (February 24, 2004).

# Glossary

**agent**—Someone who is authorized to conduct business on an author's behalf, negotiating contracts, selling rights, etc.

***Analog***—One of the premier short-fiction magazines in the science fiction genre.

**apostle**—One of the leaders of the Church of Jesus Christ of Latter-day Saints. In Mormon belief, the apostles are prophets, receiving divine revelation and inspiration.

**Book of Mormon**—In Mormon belief, a scriptural record of God's dealings with the inhabitants of ancient America, translated by Joseph Smith from divinely provided gold plates in 1830.

**cerebral palsy**—Paralysis resulting from abnormal development of or damage to the brain before birth or in the first years of life.

**characterization**—The representation in fiction or drama of human character or motives.

**dramatization**—Converting a novel or short story to script format (i.e., for stage or screen).

**freelance writer**—A person who writes for many different publications or employers.

**gospel**—Literally, "good news"—specifically, the good news that Jesus came to save humanity from its sins.

**Hugo Award**—The premier award in the science fiction field, nominated and voted on by members of the World Science Fiction Convention.

**missionary**—A ministry commissioned by a religious organization to spread the faith or carry on humanitarian work.

**Mormon**—A member of the Church of Jesus Christ of Latter-day Saints, headquartered in Salt Lake City, Utah.

**Nebula Award**—A major science fiction award nominated for and voted on by members of the Science Fiction and Fantasy Writers of America.

**novelette**—For the purposes of science fiction awards, a novel is any work of fiction 40,000 words or longer; a novella is a work of fiction 17,500 to 39,999 words long, and a novelette is 7,500 to 17,499 words long. Anything shorter than that is a short story.

**novelization**—Turning a script into a novel.

**prolific**—Very inventive or productive.

**SFWA**—The Science Fiction and Fantasy Writers of America, a professional writers' organization founded in 1966.

**ward**—A local congregation of the Church of Jesus Christ of Latter-day Saints.

# Selected Works of Orson Scott Card

1979 *Capitol*
*Hot Sleep*
*A Planet Called Treason*

1980 *Songmaster*

1981 *Unaccompanied Sonata and Other Stories*

1983 *Hart's Hope*
*The Worthing Chronicle*

1984 *A Woman of Destiny*

1985 *Ender's Game*

1986 *Speaker for the Dead*

1987 *Seventh Son: Tales of Alvin Maker, Book I*
*Wyrms*

1988 *Red Prophet: The Tales of Alvin Maker II*
*Saints*
*Characters & Viewpoint*
*Treason*

1989 *Prentice Alvin: Tales of Alvin Maker, Book III*
*The Folk of the Fringe*
*The Abyss*

1990 *How to Write Science Fiction and Fantasy*
*Maps in a Mirror: The Short Fiction of Orson Scott Card*

| | |
|---|---|
| 1991 | *Xenocide* |
| 1992 | *The Memory of Earth: Homecoming, Volume I* |
| | *Lost Boys* |
| 1993 | *The Call of Earth: Homecoming, Volume II* |
| | *A Storyteller in Zion: Essays and Speeches* |
| 1994 | *The Ships of Earth: Homecoming, Volume III* |
| | *Lovelock: The Mayflower Trilogy, Book I* |
| 1995 | *Earthfall: Homecoming, Volume IV* |
| | *Earthborn: Homecoming, Volume V* |
| | *Alvin Journeyman: Tales of Alvin Maker, IV* |
| 1996 | *Pastwatch: The Redemption of Christopher Columbus* |
| | *Children of the Mind* |
| | *Treasure Box* |
| 1997 | *Stone Tables* |
| 1998 | *Homebody* |
| | *Heartfire: The Tales of Alvin Maker V* |
| 1999 | *Enchantment* |
| | *Magic Mirror* |
| | *Ender's Shadow* |
| 2000 | *Sarah* |
| 2001 | *Shadow of the Hegemon* |
| | *Rebekah* |
| 2002 | *Shadow Puppets* |
| 2003 | *The Crystal City: The Tales of Alvin Maker VI* |
| 2004 | *Rachel & Leah* |
| 2005 | *Shadow of the Giant* |
| | *Magic Street* |

# Further Reading

## Books

Card, Orson Scott. *A Storyteller in Zion: Essays and Speeches*. Salt Lake City, Utah: Bookcraft, 1993.

Card, Orson Scott. *How to Write Science Fiction and Fantasy*. Cincinnati, Ohio: Writer's Digest Books, July 1990.

Collings, Michael R. *Storyteller: The Official Orson Scott Card Bibliography and Guide*. Woodstock, Ga.: Overlook Connection Press, 2001.

Tyson, Edith S. *Orson Scott Card: Writer of the Terrible Choice*. Lanham, Md.: Scarecrow Press, Inc., 2003.

## Internet Addresses

**Hatrack River—The Official Web Site of Orson Scott Card**
http://www.hatrack.com

**Orson Scott Card's Intergalactic Medicine Show**
http://www.oscigms.com

**The Science Fiction and Fantasy Writers of America**
http://www.sfwa.org

# Index